# Dolphins
# Their Life and Survival

# DOLPHINS
# THEIR LIFE AND SURVIVAL

Michael Donoghue &
Annie Wheeler

**BLANDFORD**
in association with
David Bateman, Auckland

# ACKNOWLEDGEMENTS

Many groups and individuals throughout the world are already working for the protection of dolphins and small whales. The authors thank in particular Earthtrust, Greenpeace, The Environmental Protection Agency and Monitor for their help in the preparation of this book.

Thanks also to the photographers and others who helped with information or photographs, in particular Bob Talbot, Sam LaBudde, Dexter Cate, Bill Perrin, Ewan Fordyce, Sean Whyte; Allan Thornton and Nick Carter of Environmental Investigation Agency; Michael Bailey, Don and Suzie White of Earthtrust; Stephen Dawson, Brian Coffey, Stephen Leatherwood, Craig van Note, Wade Doak, Stan Butler, Richard Ferraro, Ed Robinson, Lorna MacKinnon, Barbara Todd, Koen Van Waerebeek, James Watt, Mike Bradstock and Kim Westerskov. Special thanks to Kate and Morgan for their unwavering support and encouragement.

# DEDICATION

This book is dedicated to Veronica Black and her children Chloe and Anna, who died tragically before publication. Veronica was a tireless advocate for the environment, and her life continues to be an inspiration to many.

This paperback edition first published in UK 1994 by **Blandford**, A Cassell Imprint, Cassell Plc, Villiers House, 41/47 Strand London, WC2N 5JE, in association with David Bateman Ltd, "Golden Heights", 32-34 View Road, Glenfield, Auckland 10, New Zealand

**British Library Cataloguing in Publication Data**
Donoghue, Michael
    Dolphins
    1. Dolphins
    1. Title
    599.53

    ISBN 0-7137-2400-5 Paperback

Illustrations by Pat Altman
Maps by Paradigm
Typeset by Bryan Coppersmith
Printed and bound in Hong Kong
Cover photograph: James Watt

# CONTENTS

# FOREWORD by Ian Stewart

*Former Chairman of the International Whaling Commission (1986–88)*

While the attention of the world has been focused on preserving the remnants of the once-abundant whale stocks, another tragedy has been unfolding for their smaller and largely unnoticed relatives, the dolphins. Although a number of dedicated individuals have sought to draw attention to the mounting disaster, the international community has still not approached the problem in any effective way.

The threats to the dolphins' existence are many and varied, and touch on so many national and commercial interests that reports tend to be placed in the "too-hard" basket. Whereas the near extinction of the great whales took centuries to achieve, modern fishing techniques coupled with pollution and degradation of the marine environment seem likely to produce a similar result for the small cetaceans within a few decades – that is, within our own lifetimes. Sadly, it seems that the world has learned little from its experience with the whales, and that a species has to become endangered and at the risk of disappearing altogether from our planet before international action can be mobilised to preserve its existence.

Although direct catching has made serious inroads into certain dolphin stocks, it is ironic that the greatest depletion – at least 6 million animals over 30 years – has been brought about as an incidental (but not accidental) aspect of fishing for yellowfin tuna in the eastern Pacific. Deaths from this cause are still continuing at the rate of 125,000 or more per year. Mortality from drift-net fishing is undoubtedly high, too, and pollution of rivers, coastal waters, and the high seas has rendered whole habitats unfit for marine life. Overfishing has at the same time reduced the food supply. All told, the prospects for survival are stacked against the dolphins.

The problem is a global one, and can be successfully tackled only at the international level. There is no existing international agency with the mandate or the resources to deal with all aspects. It would assist greatly, however, if one agency would accept the prime responsibility for dolphins and their survival, seeking then to stimulate and co-ordinate action by other agencies in specific areas of interest. The International Whaling Commission (IWC) would seem to be the logical body to step into the breach by extending its managerial and conservation functions to cover all species of cetaceans. Unfortunately, apart from carrying out limited scientific studies, the IWC has been prevented by essentially political reasons from even discussing the question of the smaller cetaceans, much less taking action on their behalf. This situation is largely but not entirely related to sensitivities on the part of certain member governments over the exercise of sovereignty by states in 200-mile zones.

In this comprehensive survey Michael Donoghue and Annie Wheeler have brought together a wealth of useful information about dolphins' characteristics and habitats, as well as the state of the stocks of the many different species. They set out in grim detail the threats they face. It all adds up to a strong plea to the international community to take notice and act before it becomes too late.

# INTRODUCTION

Dolphins speak in ways we have not yet learned to understand. They perceive the world in ways that are beyond the scope of our senses, and their sense of sound is finer and more sophisticated than that of the greatest human musician. A dolphin's brain size and complexity is equivalent to that of a human, and they are undoubtedly highly intelligent, humorous and social beings. We have the opportunity to meet and interact with dolphins in the wild, to learn what they have to teach. They frequently extend the invitation, and have done so over the centuries, unfailingly treating us with extreme gentleness and goodwill – anyone who has met dolphins on the ocean, or joined them in the sea, knows how playful and friendly they are. We are only beginning to discover the possibilities for interspecies communication.

Our encounters with dolphins and what we have discovered of their world and reality form part of this story. But the remainder is a cry for help, help to save the dolphins. For this is also the story of their plight. Much of it is a tragic and often cruel and senseless story, which we hope will help awaken sufficient public outrage and action to ensure that the slaughter of these peaceful and intelligent creatures is urgently halted.

Every year, a million or even more dolphins and porpoises are killed throughout the world. They are being deliberately hunted for human food, to be made into fertiliser or chicken food, or to be used as crab bait. Others are being "accidentally" caught and killed in fishing nets – an estimated half a million to a million dolphins and small whales are dying annually as a result of getting entangled in modern gill-nets used by the fishing industry. The tuna-fishing industry deliberately sets its nets around schools of dolphins to try to catch the tuna fish swimming beneath, and in the process kills tens of thousands of dolphins. In some parts of the world, dolphins are still being hunted for sport, or because fishermen think they are stealing or scaring away their fish, or because their sexual organs are considered to have magical qualities.

A few species are already on the verge of extinction. The most critically endangered are the rare river dolphins of South America, China, India, Nepal, and Pakistan. These animals have adapted to a very specialised river environment and are extremely vulnerable to destruction of their habitat as a result of industrial development and increasing human population with its attendant pollution. The Yangtze River dolphin, (or baiji), and Indus River dolphin – strange, almost blind creatures that are among the most primitive of dolphin species – now number only in their hundreds. As destruction of their river homes continues, their chances for survival look more and more grim. Unless urgent action is taken they could well be extinct by early next century.

The coastal seas around heavily industrialised areas are becoming increasingly fouled with toxic waste and chemical pollutants and this, too, is wiping out large numbers of dolphins. Because of their coastal habitat and position at the top of the food chain, many dolphin species have accumulated considerable levels of industrial poisons. In the Baltic Sea this has drastically reduced the numbers of harbour porpoises. The white whales or belugas of the St Lawrence River in Canada are so loaded with industrial toxins they are declared dangerous toxic waste themselves when they die, and the St Lawrence beluga appears to be doomed no matter how quickly its environment is cleaned up. Because many victims of industrial pollutants die at sea, the true number affected will never be known. The combination of

"With no technology, no art, no scientific achievements, one might ask, for what purpose did the cetaceans evolve their large cerebral cortex through the past ten million years?

"One answer might be that dolphins have evolved to enjoy the pleasure of simply being alive . . .

"And when the day comes that we can communicate intelligently with dolphins, they may introduce us to the concept of survival without aggression, and the true joy of living, which at present eludes us."

*Horace Dobbs,*
*British conservationist*

global warming and the increasing damage being done to the ozone layer may have profound effects on ocean productivity, currents, and upwellings, and hence on the abundance and distribution of many marine species.

Because dolphins and porpoises are of no great economic value to most developed nations, except Japan, little research has been carried out on their distribution and abundance. Few reliable records exist of past populations, and the status of many dolphin populations is difficult to assess accurately. But we know for certain that human intervention over the past 20 years has slashed dolphin populations drastically, either locally or throughout their range.

Where dolphins are deliberately hunted, and their meat is sold, trade figures mean that a reasonably accurate picture can usually be drawn of the human impacts on population numbers. Information on the impacts of coastal gill-netting, oceanic drift-netting or industrial pollution is, however, far less complete. Because so much net fishing is carried out without independent observers, tens or even hundreds of thousands of accidental drownings each year undoubtedly go unreported.

"Save the Whales" has been a catchphrase for the last two decades and world attention has focussed on the need to protect the great whales. Conservationists have repeatedly confronted the whalers both on the high seas and in the conference rooms of the International Whaling Commission, the international regulatory body for the whaling industry. By 1982, a ban on commercial whaling was achieved which has succeeded in greatly reducing the number of whales hunted and killed. But meanwhile the massacre of dolphins, porpoises, and small whales has been continuing unabated. At present, over five times as many dolphins and small whales are being killed each year as the number of great whales that were being killed at the height of the whaling industry. And to date no international, and very few national, agreements or agencies are specifically charged with ensuring the protection of dolphins, porpoises and small cetaceans.

# 1:    THE MOST THREATENED SPECIES

This section describes species of dolphins, porpoises and small whales that have been most heavily affected by human activities in recent years and whose survival is most threatened. They are grouped into four categories: those in imminent danger of extinction; those which are threatened with a similar fate unless present trends are reversed; those which have been significantly depleted in some part or parts of their range; and those for which there is insufficient information to make a confident assessment. Some species are being killed in their thousands. For species that are already less abundant than that, even small losses may threaten their very survival.

Each species' ranking according to CITES (Convention on International Trade in Endangered Species – see Chapter 14) is also given.

## 1.  SPECIES ON THE VERGE OF EXTINCTION

### Yangtze River dolphin (baiji)

Found only in restricted areas of the Yangtze River in China. Thought to be reduced in number to no more than 150. Population continuing to decline owing to loss of habitat, pollution and accidental catch in rolling hook fishery. Probably the most endangered cetacean in the world.
**CITES listing: Highly endangered.**

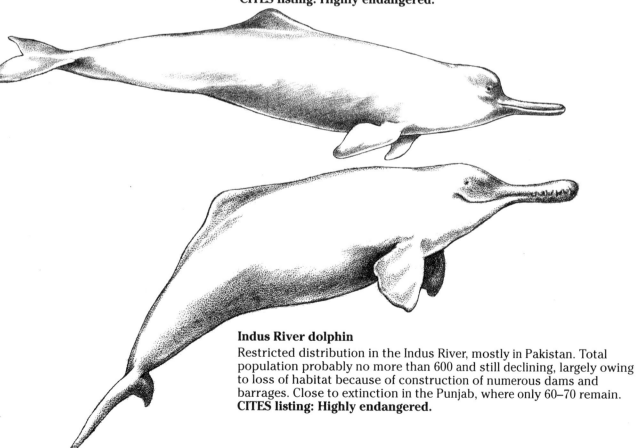

### Indus River dolphin

Restricted distribution in the Indus River, mostly in Pakistan. Total population probably no more than 600 and still declining, largely owing to loss of habitat because of construction of numerous dams and barrages. Close to extinction in the Punjab, where only 60–70 remain.
**CITES listing: Highly endangered.**

**Gulf of California harbour porpoise (vaquita or cochito)**

Confined to shallow water in the northern Gulf of California in Mexico. Probably never common. Present numbers unknown, but certainly very low – only 47 confirmed records of the animal are reliably reported. Severely affected by coastal gill-net fishery in the 1970s. Still taken occasionally in gill-nets and shrimp trawls. Probably the most endangered marine cetacean.
**CITES listing: Highly endangered.**

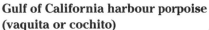

## 2. SPECIES WHOSE SURVIVAL IS THREATENED

**Ganges River dolphin (Ganges susu)**

Probably still several thousand animals left, but found only in the Ganges River and its tributaries, which are being continually degraded by pressures of development. Dams and pollution of the river threaten the long-term survival of the remaining dolphins, which are also still hunted for their oil.
**CITES listing: Endangered if trade is not regulated.**

**Amazon River dolphin (boto or boutu)**

Population status unknown, but thought to number only a few thousand animals, scattered throughout the Amazon basin. Long-term future in doubt, owing to increasing destruction of habitat through dams, logging, mining, increased river traffic, and hunting. Entanglement in fishing nets is the latest hazard.
**CITES listing: Highly endangered.**

### Chilean black dolphin

Restricted to the southern waters of Chile and Tierra del Fuego, this rare dolphin has been extensively hunted to provide bait for crab pots for the southern king crab fishery. Catches of several thousand have been reported in recent years, and the population could be critically endangered.
**CITES listing: Highly endangered.**

### Commerson's dolphin

Also a popular bait for crab pots. The Tierra del Fuego population of this rare species has been drastically reduced. The only place where the dolphin is still found in reasonable numbers is the remote Kerguelen Islands in the sub-antarctic Indian Ocean.
**CITES listing: Highly endangered.**

### Harbour porpoise

Once abundant and widely distributed throughout the Northern Hemisphere, populations of the harbour porpoise have slumped over the past two decades because of human activities. In the 1970s, thousands of porpoises drowned in drift-nets in the North Atlantic, and in the Black Sea, an estimated 10,000 or more per year were shot by hunters. The Baltic and North Sea populations have almost vanished because of pollution, and entanglement in set-nets has drastically reduced the numbers of porpoises in the Bay of Fundy and off the California coast. In Greenland, porpoises are still an important part of the diet, and approximately 1000 animals are reported to be taken each year. The porpoise is practically extinct in Japan, largely because of overexploitation in the past.
**CITES listing: Endangered if trade is not regulated.**

### Peale's dolphin

This dolphin is another victim of the Chilean king crab fishery. The number killed in recent years is uncertain, but surveys indicate that the population declined significantly between 1979 and 1982. The dolphin's range is restricted to the southern tip of South America, and the killing of perhaps thousands of animals in the past decade is a matter of grave concern.
**CITES listing: Endangered if trade is not regulated.**

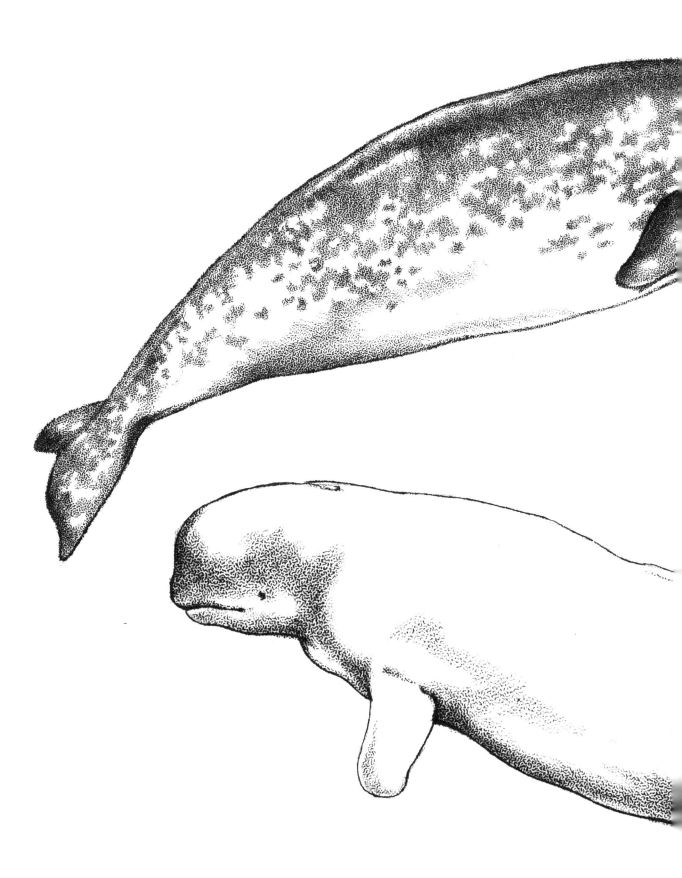

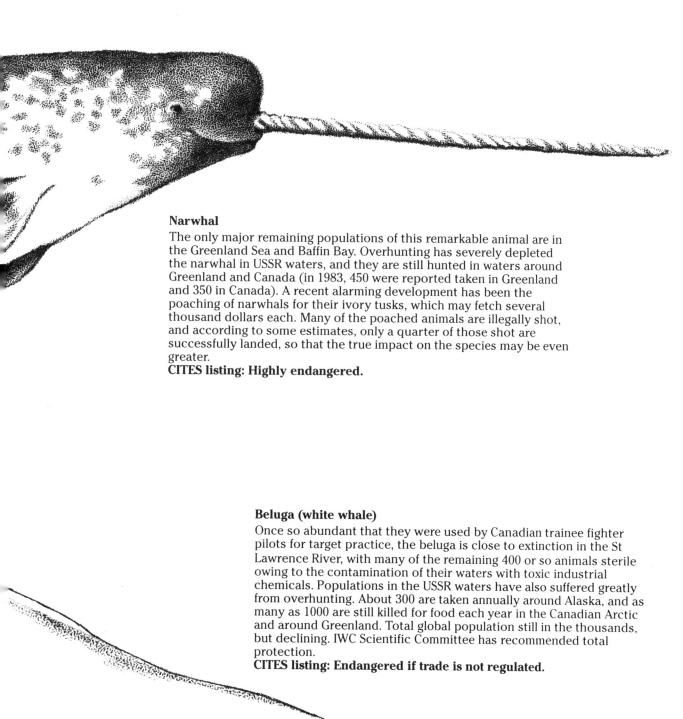

### Narwhal

The only major remaining populations of this remarkable animal are in the Greenland Sea and Baffin Bay. Overhunting has severely depleted the narwhal in USSR waters, and they are still hunted in waters around Greenland and Canada (in 1983, 450 were reported taken in Greenland and 350 in Canada). A recent alarming development has been the poaching of narwhals for their ivory tusks, which may fetch several thousand dollars each. Many of the poached animals are illegally shot, and according to some estimates, only a quarter of those shot are successfully landed, so that the true impact on the species may be even greater.

**CITES listing: Highly endangered.**

### Beluga (white whale)

Once so abundant that they were used by Canadian trainee fighter pilots for target practice, the beluga is close to extinction in the St Lawrence River, with many of the remaining 400 or so animals sterile owing to the contamination of their waters with toxic industrial chemicals. Populations in the USSR waters have also suffered greatly from overhunting. About 300 are taken annually around Alaska, and as many as 1000 are still killed for food each year in the Canadian Arctic and around Greenland. Total global population still in the thousands, but declining. IWC Scientific Committee has recommended total protection.

**CITES listing: Endangered if trade is not regulated.**

# 3. SPECIES SIGNIFICANTLY REDUCED IN AT LEAST PART OF THEIR RANGE

## Common dolphin

Widely distributed throughout the world, the common dolphin suffers from a number of conflicts with fisheries, which may be accounting for as many as 10,000 dolphins each year. Many dolphins die in the purse-seine nets of the tuna fleet in the Eastern Tropical Pacific (ETP), and tens of thousands more die each year in drift-nets in the North and South Pacific and the Mediterranean Sea. Coastal gill-nets take a large toll worldwide (including shark nets to protect bathers in South Africa). Tens of thousands of dolphins were gunned down in the Black Sea each year until hunting stopped in 1984.
**CITES listing: Endangered if trade is not regulated.**

## Bottlenose dolphin

The dolphin best known to most humans and the most common performer at oceanaria and marinelands (over half of the dolphins taken to be kept in captivity have been bottlenose). Also the dolphin species most favoured for use by the military. Worldwide distribution, but affected by human activities throughout its range. The Black Sea population was almost wiped out by hunters, and in Japanese waters thousands have died in drive fisheries, particularly at Iki Island. As many as 15,000 may have drowned in drift nets in the Arafura and Timor Seas before Australian authorities banned the use of large drift nets in 1986. Frequently reported drowned in coastal gill-nets. Exact number of annual deaths in set-nets each year unknown, but probably several thousand.
**CITES listing: Endangered if trade not regulated.**

## Striped dolphin

Favoured for human consumption in southern Japan and target of many of the drives – as many as 3000 dolphins have been killed in a single drive. Frequent victim of coastal gill-nets, especially in tropical waters.
**CITES listing: Endangered if trade not regulated.**

### Spinner dolphin
Several sub-species heavily reduced in numbers by the yellowfin tuna purse-seine fishery. Hundreds of thousands of animals killed in recent years.
**CITES listing: Endangered if trade not regulated.**

### Spotted dolphin
Most heavily affected species in the ETP purse-seine tuna fishery. Severely depleted since the 1960s, when purse seining began, and between 30 and 50 per cent of original population size. High mortality rate of mature females in recent years is cause for concern.
**CITES listing: Endangered if trade not regulated.**

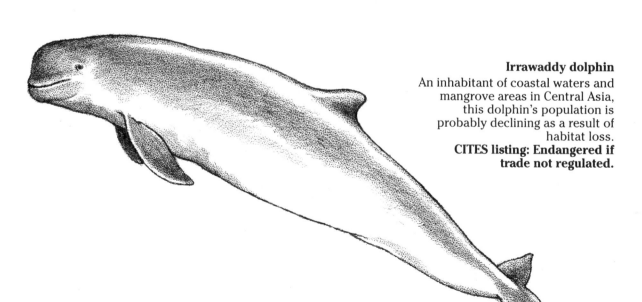

### Irrawaddy dolphin
An inhabitant of coastal waters and mangrove areas in Central Asia, this dolphin's population is probably declining as a result of habitat loss.
**CITES listing: Endangered if trade not regulated.**

### Risso's dolphin

Distributed throughout the world, this dolphin falls victim to gill-nets, especially around Sri Lanka, where many die annually. Also taken in drives at Iki Island.
**CITES listing: Endangered if trade not regulated.**

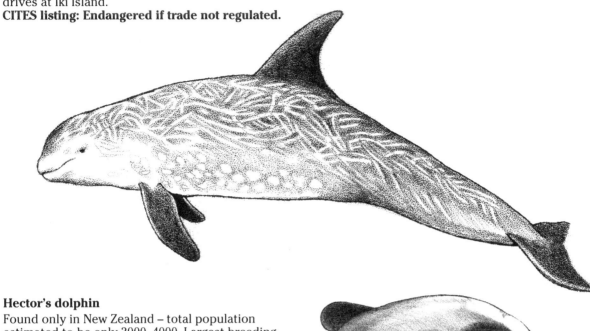

### Hector's dolphin

Found only in New Zealand – total population estimated to be only 3000–4000. Largest breeding group of some 740 dolphins lost at least 230 members to gill-net entanglement between 1984 and 1988.
**CITES listing: Endangered if trade not regulated.**

### Dusky dolphin

Found only in New Zealand, South Africa and South America. A directed fishery in Peru took some 10,000 dolphins each year for human consumption, mainly by the use of small drift-nets during the 1980s. Population status uncertain, but South American population undoubtedly greatly reduced.
**CITES listing: Endangered if trade not regulated.**

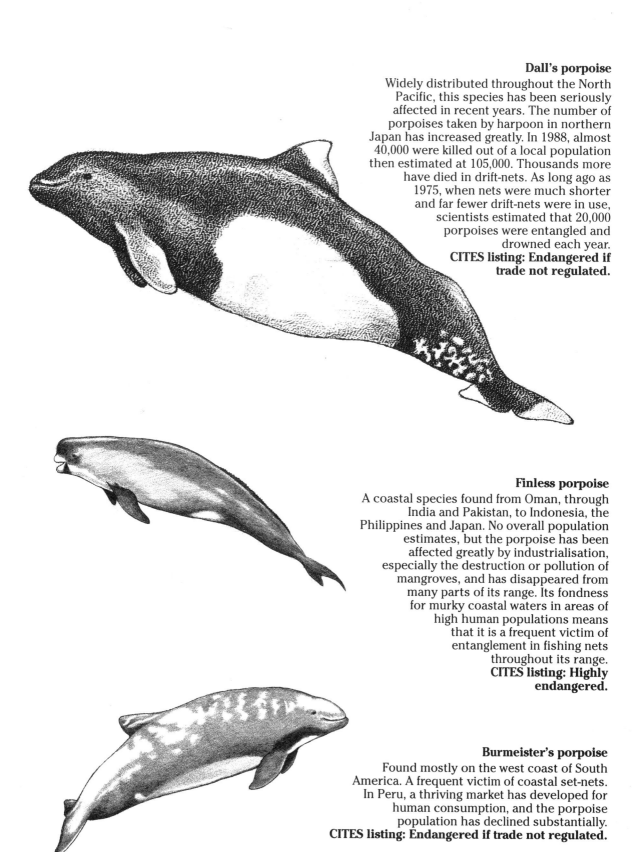

### Dall's porpoise
Widely distributed throughout the North Pacific, this species has been seriously affected in recent years. The number of porpoises taken by harpoon in northern Japan has increased greatly. In 1988, almost 40,000 were killed out of a local population then estimated at 105,000. Thousands more have died in drift-nets. As long ago as 1975, when nets were much shorter and far fewer drift-nets were in use, scientists estimated that 20,000 porpoises were entangled and drowned each year.
**CITES listing: Endangered if trade not regulated.**

### Finless porpoise
A coastal species found from Oman, through India and Pakistan, to Indonesia, the Philippines and Japan. No overall population estimates, but the porpoise has been affected greatly by industrialisation, especially the destruction or pollution of mangroves, and has disappeared from many parts of its range. Its fondness for murky coastal waters in areas of high human populations means that it is a frequent victim of entanglement in fishing nets throughout its range.
**CITES listing: Highly endangered.**

### Burmeister's porpoise
Found mostly on the west coast of South America. A frequent victim of coastal set-nets. In Peru, a thriving market has developed for human consumption, and the porpoise population has declined substantially.
**CITES listing: Endangered if trade not regulated.**

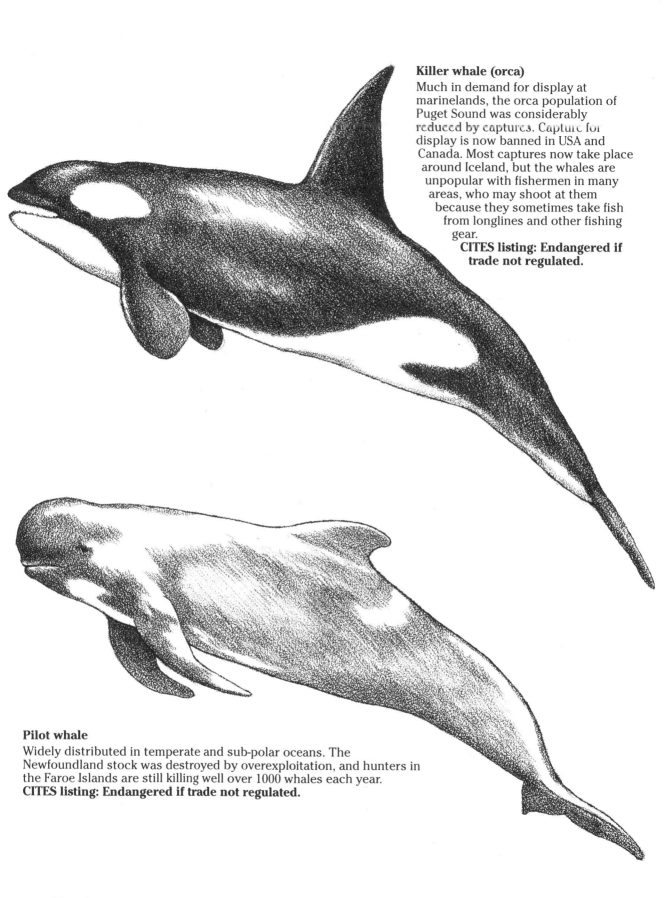

**Killer whale (orca)**
Much in demand for display at marinelands, the orca population of Puget Sound was considerably reduced by captures. Capture for display is now banned in USA and Canada. Most captures now take place around Iceland, but the whales are unpopular with fishermen in many areas, who may shoot at them because they sometimes take fish from longlines and other fishing gear.
**CITES listing: Endangered if trade not regulated.**

**Pilot whale**
Widely distributed in temperate and sub-polar oceans. The Newfoundland stock was destroyed by overexploitation, and hunters in the Faroe Islands are still killing well over 1000 whales each year.
**CITES listing: Endangered if trade not regulated.**

# 4. SPECIES FOR WHICH INFORMATION IS INSUFFICIENT

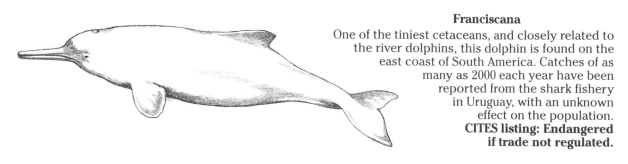

### Franciscana
One of the tiniest cetaceans, and closely related to the river dolphins, this dolphin is found on the east coast of South America. Catches of as many as 2000 each year have been reported from the shark fishery in Uruguay, with an unknown effect on the population.
**CITES listing: Endangered if trade not regulated.**

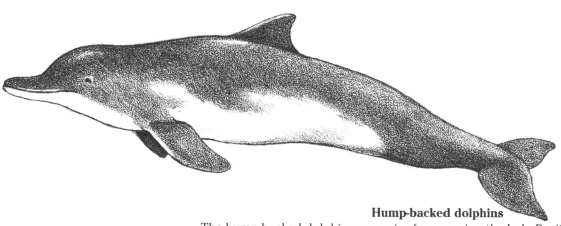

### Hump-backed dolphins
The hump-backed dolphins comprise four species: the Indo-Pacific and Atlantic hump-backed dolphins, the rough-toothed dolphin and the tucuxi. Their favoured habitats of rivers, estuaries, and coastal zones expose them to the effects of pollution and habitat destruction. Little scientific study has been carried out to assess their present status.
**CITES listing: Highly endangered.**

### Heaviside's dolphin
Found around the coasts of Namibia and South Africa, where it is often caught in gill-nets. Population status uncertain.
**CITES listing: Endangered if trade not regulated.**

# PART ONE

Humans have a special affinity for dolphins, which are widely perceived as having a special degree of intelligence. In fact, the sperm whale (one of the toothed whales) boasts the largest brain on the planet, and in many dolphins, the arrangement and complexity of the brain and nervous system show striking similarities to those of humans. The small cetaceans (dolphins, porpoises, and small toothed whales) show a remarkable range of adaptations to life in and under the surface of the ocean.

---

# 2:  THE HUMAN/DOLPHIN ENCOUNTER

Dolphins are very much in vogue these days. They have become a symbol, along with rainbows, of the dawning of a new age of Aquarius, when qualities of love, peace, and harmony have their renaissance on the earth. Our cousins in the sea, as they are sometimes called, seem to us to have created a society far closer to human ideals of Utopia than anything we have managed to achieve on land, and their social behaviour and lifestyle embody many of the virtues and qualities we humans hold so dear. No wonder, then, that we make of them a symbol of our own visionary dreams. Their movement in the oceans speaks to us of freedom, grace and beauty. Their lifestyle contains all the ingredients that for us make up "the good life" – plenty of time devoted to playing, socialising, and making love. Their society is co-operative, with many examples of seemingly altruistic behaviour, and dolphins are always ready to come to the assistance of those in distress, both their own species and humans. Apart from a few minor displays, they are free of aggression toward their own kind. "It is with a feeling of surprise and wonder, even of awe, that humans become aware of a great intelligence living in the sea; of marine mammals with a perception greater than that of other animals, more akin to our own," says New Zealander Frank Robson, who has spent many years working with dolphins both in captivity and in the wild. "We see them communicating easily with one another, trying to communicate with us, solving problems, reasoning, enjoying a joke."

The ancient Mediterranean cultures believed that the dolphin represented the vital power of the sea. Delphys, the Greek word for dolphin, means womb. Dolphins were closely linked with the gods, and were a complex symbol associated not only with innocent love and friendship, beauty and harmony, and erotic love, but also with darker areas of death and destruction. Popularly considered to be a creature of peaceful virtue and undisguised joy, the dolphin was a guardian of the sea and a guide to other worlds. In these times, killing a dolphin was tantamount to killing a person, and both crimes were punished with the death penalty.

Early Greek mythology describes several encounters between a strong god/hero and a snake/dolphin/woman figure. One of the most famous is that of the Sun God Apollo, who fought with Delphyne, the dolphin/womb monster. When he defeated her he founded an oracle in the dolphins' honour at Delphi (dolphin town), building a shrine where he hoped humans might be guided by a sense of otherworldliness. He also instituted a festival called Delphinia to commemorate his victory. A God had the power to turn himself into whoever or whatever he

"If we comb through our stories and our encounters with wild whales and dolphins, we find that they seem to hang together along a shining thread - that whales and dolphins know what they are doing, that their actions are purposeful, and stunningly specific to the occasion, that they intend us no harm, that they are aware."

*Joan McIntyre,*
*Canadian conservationist*

defeated or ate, so Apollo could now assume the form of a dolphin. Once, while in a giant dolphin body, Apollo commandeered a boat full of merchants and redirected their craft to Delphi. There he revealed himself as god and ordered them to serve him as priests in his new shrine.

Dolphins not only guided the god of the sea, Poseidon, to his lover Amphitrite, but also persuaded her to marry him. Poseidon was so grateful that he created a constellation in the dolphins' honour called Delphinus, just west of Pegasus. The son of Poseidon and Amphitrite was called Triton, and was usually represented as half-man, half-dolphin, holding in his left hand an upright dolphin that suggests an erect penis. Triton roamed the shores raping anyone who took his fancy and earned himself the title Sea Satyr. Men used to wear dolphin tails and dance in his honour.

Dolphins graced mosaics, ceramics, and painted murals in ancient Greek and Roman societies. Some of the earliest images are of leaping and swimming dolphins that feature on painted frescoes in the Minoan temple of Knossos on Crete, dating back over 3000 years to when the Minoan civilisation ruled much of the Mediterranean. Frequently a symbol of salvation, a dolphin talisman would ensure a safe journey on land or at sea, and its image stamped on a coin or token was used as a good luck charm. Dolphins were often associated with the anchor, another symbol of salvation, and a dolphin twined around an anchor signified arrested speed, or prudence.

The dolphin rider is another image that occurs frequently in early Mediterranean mythology. Eros and Aphrodite were the most popular dolphin riders, and their relationship with the dolphins they rode appears sensuous, loving and often erotic. There is also evidence that not only gods and mythical figures were associated with dolphins and mounted their backs, but children apparently rode wild dolphins in just about every bay, harbour, and inlet of the ancient Mediterranean, and dolphins often befriended sailors and rescued people from the sea, carrying them safely to land.

A popular legend tells of Arion, a lyric poet and musician, who was returning to Greece from Italy, laden with riches he had won at music competitions. The crew of the boat on which he was travelling attacked and were about to kill him when he asked for a last favour – to play a tune. The sound of his music attracted a school of dolphins, whereupon Arion leapt overboard and was carried safely to shore on the back of one of the dolphins. In his gratitude, he erected a bronze statue of a dolphin rider on the clifftops, honouring Poseidon, God of the Sea.

In the Pacific, just as in ancient Greece and Rome, dolphins have been traditionally regarded as messengers of the gods. Ancestral spirits were believed to take the form of guardian dolphins or sharks, who guided canoes, effected rescues, and assisted in fishing.

A tribe of Aborigines known as the Dolphin People, who live on Mornington Island in the Gulf of Carpentaria, in northern Australia, is said to have been in direct communication for thousands of years with the wild bottlenose dolphins who reside just off the coast. The Dolphin People shamans know a complex series of whistles that signal the dolphins to venture close to shore. The whistling then becomes animated, before stopping altogether. The shamans explain that, at that point, they begin to speak to the dolphins mind to mind.

In Kiribati in the Pacific Ocean, formerly known as the Gilbert Islands, certain local clans also had the power of dolphin calling. A dolphin caller would go into a dream where his spirit went out of his body and sought the dolphin folk in their home under the western horizon and invited them to a dance, with feasting, in the village. If he spoke the words of the invitation correctly, the dolphins would follow him with cries of joy to the surface. Having led them to the lagoon

"The Maori once regarded the dolphin as some kind of God or influence to direct them to things they wanted to know. To me it is a human being in the sea.... We only call dolphins when we need help in a rough sea, or we are in difficulty or if there is something we would like to know about relatives at a distance over the ocean. If a relative is sick when the dolphin appears it will give a sign whether or not that person will recover or has already recovered. We can tell from the way it leaps."

*Waipu Pita,*
*contemporary Maori elder*
*New Zealand*

entrance, the caller would fly forward to rejoin his body and warn the people of the coming of "our friends from the west". This ritual was practised until the last decade or so but has apparently now ceased, which is perhaps in the best interests of the dolphins. They often finished up as the main item on the menu at the feast after their visit.

New Zealand's indigenous Maori people also had an active relationship with dolphins and called them with the word "Tepuhi", which emulates the sound a dolphin makes blowing air through its breathing hole.

Around the world, many cultures believe that any harm done to a dolphin may cause ill-fortune or sickness. In the Ganges, Amazon, and other major rivers inhabited by freshwater dolphins, similar protective myths have arisen, often coupled with symbiotic fishing practices. Mutual assistance in fishing is a widespread human/dolphin relationship that has now been well documented in both North Africa and Brazil. Fishermen on the south coast of France and from the Solomon Islands are both credited with the power to call dolphins from the sea.

Solitary dophins have been known to spend long periods around human settlements, encounters which attest to their humour, playfulness, curiosity and gentleness, and their readiness to help humans in distress.

One of the earliest documented encounters took place in AD 109 when a dolphin befriended a boy swimming offshore at the Roman settlement of Hippo in northern Africa, and thereafter returned day after day to play with other children, who slowly overcame their initial fear. However, the expense of welcoming and entertaining all the visitors who came to see the dolphin began to tax the modest resources of the town, and to destroy its quiet and peaceful character. In the end, according to the classical writer Pliny, it was "decided to do away secretly with the cause of the invasion."

The first account of a solitary dolphin encounter since classical times seems to be in England in 1814. A 4-metre (13-foot) male bottlenose called Gabriel made his home in the river Dart and befriended children and adults. Some entrepreneurial showmen then decided they would try to make money out of his popularity and they caught him with the hope of transporting him to London to put on display. Gabriel died an agonising death on the back of a cart on his way to London.

A happier story is that of Pelorus Jack, a dolphin who escorted a ferry steamer through New Zealand's narrow French Pass for some 24 years from 1888 to 1912. Thought to be a Risso's dolphin, he would meet steamers with faithful regularity, joining and leaving at a particular spot, and then bow riding at speeds up to 15 knots and rubbing his body against the ship's hull. Pelorus Jack became famous throughout the world and attracted thousands of tourists. Eventually public concern for his safety persuaded the New Zealand Government of the day to introduce special protective legislation. The need for such protection for friendly dolphins is evident in the stories of Opo and Nina, who both suffered fates similar to that of the Hippo dolphin.

## OPO AND NINA

In 1955 a solitary bottlenose dolphin came to live in the remote Hokianga Harbour in Northland, New Zealand, and was soon to cause a sensation. Throughout the summer the dolphin, who came to be known as Opo, played with swimmers, performed tricks, escorted boats in the harbour, and for 11 weeks received regular newspaper coverage. Opo developed a special friendship with a 12-year-old girl, who would enter the water five or six times a day to swim with or stand and talk to her. Opo would ease between her legs and take her for rides.

An increasing number of people flocked to visit Opo, with 1500 visitors sometimes crowding the beach. Locals began to fear for her safety. Indeed several attempts were made on her life, until finally one day she was found dead on the rocks, thought to have been killed by gelignite.

On the other side of the world on the north-west coast of Spain, a dolphin called Nina created a similar social upheaval in 1972. At first befriending a local diver, Nina then attracted a Cousteau film team and her fame spread until she soon became a Spanish national heroine. She made a fuss of every boat that approached her and mixed with all bathers on the beach, allowing them to pet her, hold her tail, and ride on her back. As many as 2000 people would throng into the water to touch her. For five months tourists flocked to the area, creating traffic jams and increasing resentment from some of the locals. Concern for her safety grew and laws were passed for her protection. But one day, like Opo, her dead body was found washed ashore, and human foul play was suspected.

## DONALD

Donald first made his appearance when he started playing and interacting with divers near a marine laboratory on the Isle of Man in 1972. Encounters with Donald were documented for the next 6 years, during which time he travelled on a southward odyssey along some 480 km (300 miles) of British coastline, from the Isle of Man to Wales and then to Cornwall, stopping off in small harbours, boat havens and coves along the way to socialise. Many anecdotes about this cheeky and colourful personality have been collected and published by Horace Dobbs. Donald loved biting paddles, splashing and capsizing people and pushing boats around. The more excited people became, the more active and outrageous he would get. He would meddle with fishing nets, pull up anchors and tow boats, tease dogs and tow swimmers. He could also be very possessive, especially towards women. Dobb's book, Save the Dolphins, describes a lengthy and tender relationship that developed between Donald and a woman trainer Maura Mitchell, which included croonings and cuddles at each meeting, during which Donald would shut his eyes.

## THE MONKEY MIA DOLPHINS

Monkey Mia, on the remote western coastline of Australia, has for more than two decades been visited by wild dolphins. Dolphins of all ages and humans intermingle daily in knee-deep water in what is the longest human/dolphin encounter on record. Around 10 dolphins are usually in the bay, part of a larger group further off the coast. Their visits break many of the established patterns of human/dolphin encounter: they accept gifts of dead fish (one theory is that the dolphins receive the fish as a signal from humans that they have come to play and interact), and they maintain their own social grouping while at the same time allowing close human contact. They have provided a wonderful opportunity to get to know dolphins in the wild, and several of the females have given birth over the years they have been frequenting Monkey Mia, thus enabling study of their maternal care and child development.

As the news of Monkey Mia spread, it became one of Australia's leading tourist attractions and was included on the itinerary of tour buses. People from all over the world began to make pilgrimages to

*Dusky dolphins repeatedly practise aerial leaps
and spins, and fin and head slaps.* Barbara Todd

*Left*: Trapped striped dolphins await slaughter in Futo Harbour, southern Japan. Until recently, thousands of dolphins have been hunted and killed each year in Japanese drive fisheries. Fishermen drove groups of dolphins into narrow bays, where the herded animals were stabbed, harpooned or knifed to death. The average catch by this method between 1975 and 1986 was 4700 per year, mostly striped dolphins.  Earthtrust

*Below*: Dall's porpoises are deliberately killed in great numbers in the seas around the Iwate Prefecture, Japan. Dall's porpoises are playful creatures and delight in riding the bow waves of boats, making them easy targets for fishermen armed with harpoons. Over 10,000 of them were harpooned each year between 1976 and 1987, most ending up in fish markets.  W.F. Perrin

*Leaping dusky dolphin.* Barbara Todd

*Common dolphins riding the bow wave of a large ship.* Bob Talbot

**Above**: *Dusky dolphin, mother and calf. Mothers and young remain together for up to 8 years in some species.* Barbara Todd

**Left**: *"Porpoise fishing" is a method used for catching tuna which associate with dolphins in the Eastern Tropical Pacific. Here a purse-seiner sets its net around a school of dolphins and speedboats drive in tight circles at high speed to frighten the dolphins and tuna back into the net.* NMFS

**Left**: *Dolphins trapped in a purse-seine net. Although attempts are made by some fishing crews to free the dolphins, between 8-12 million have been killed by purse-seiners over the last 30 years.* NMFS

**Below**: *Human and dolphin meet. "Where people have behaved toward cetaceans in a benign, communicative manner, they have often met with prolonged and remarkable responses." (Wade Doak)* Bob Talbot

*First encounters with a wild dolphin are unforgettable and moving experiences for human visitors to the sea.* Stephen Leatherwood/Oceans Society Expeditions

Monkey Mia and some 200,000 visitors arrived during the 1989 season. Local residents have sought special legislation to protect the dolphins, an information centre has been built, and now full-time custodians are appointed to act as guardians and to teach the public how to treat the dolphins. As always, the mass tourist reponse carries its own breed of problems and risks. Foreign objects innocently thrown to dolphins may cause their death, as happens with dolphins in captivity. Speed boats and fishing nets also need to be kept out of the area.

## DOLPHINS COMING TO THE RESCUE

Dolphins have often rescued people at sea. Swimmers in distress have been carried to safety on dolphins' backs. Dolphins have suddenly appeared to help fight off a shark attack, and they frequently guide boats through storms or treacherous waters. Yvonne Vladislavich was on a cabin cruiser that was caught by a wave and sank off Mozambique. She swam for 40 km (25 miles) in the shark-infested Indian Ocean, but she had cut her foot and she saw half a dozen sharks trailing her. As the sharks circled closer, two dolphins appeared at her side and protected her until she reached a buoy and could climb up onto it to safety.

Another report tells of a Mrs Yvonne Bliss who fell off a boat in the West Indies. She describes how a porpoise appeared and guided her so that she was being carried with the tide, and then helped her to a section of shallow water. As soon as she was safe her rescuer "took off like a streak on down the channel".

## AND BEING RESCUED

The echolocation system of dolphins occasionally lets them down, and they become stranded on beaches. Most of the humans who have been involved in rescues of dolphins or small whales such as pilot whales will readily admit that it is an emotional and moving experience. Experiences in recent years in New Zealand and Australia suggest that many stranded animals can be saved if certain simple rules are followed.

The biggest danger for any stranded cetacean is overheating. The blubber which keeps them warm in the water acts as an overly-effective insulator on land, and they can literally cook in their own fat if they are not kept cool. The tail flukes radiate heat from the body most effectively, and they should be consistently cooled with water to avoid overheating. The animal should be kept on its belly, with as much of the body as possible covered with damp blankets or sheets to prevent the sun's rays from burning the sensitive skin.

Muscle cramps can be relieved, and the animal's sense of balance restored, by rocking a stranded dolphin or whale from side to side as the tide comes in, just before its refloating.

Stranded dolphins can sometimes be transported by helicopter from the stranding site to the open sea. When refloating a herd, it is important to hold the rescued animals together until the entire herd is assembled before releasing them to the open sea.

## PROJECT INTERLOCK

New Zealanders Wade and Jan Doak have embarked on a life-long study into the cetacean mind, called "Project Interlock". It all began when Wade was swimming with dolphins, imitating their movement in an undulation that began at the head and rippled along his body to his

An American, Chi-uh Gawain, made many journeys to Monkey Mia and wrote a book about her experiences. "I have the impression the dolphins don't want us to have any purpose in our relations with them. And especially no tricks or pretence. They want us to be ourselves and they themselves and to meet as friends . . . Only after some quiet times with a dolphin do we enjoy letting it be in charge of the encounter, and see what it may decide to do next with us."

*The ying-yang symbol painted on the hull of the Doaks' Wharram catamaran symbolises the link between humans and dolphins.*
*Wade Doak*

fins. A dolphin drew alongside, and by counter-opposing its flippers, barrel-rolled right in front of his mask. Doak imitated this corkscrew manoeuvre, albeit rather slowly and clumsily. As Doak describes, "Then something startling happened.... a formation of six dolphins abreast of me... repeated that trick in unison, reinforcing my newly acquired mimicry patterns."

With his family and friends Doak has pioneered work and communication with dolphins in the wild, interacting with them on their terms, and in their environment. Working from a base in Northland, New Zealand, Doak spends long hours at sea on a small catamaran, inviting close encounters with dolphins. When going out to meet dolphins he plays "sweet music" through the bows of the boat to create a receptive mood and establish trust. Doak also understands body language to be a key to communicating with cetaceans, and he experimented with special wetsuits that were modelled on the dolphin body, black above and white below, with both legs enclosed in a sheath terminating in a tailfin or jetfins. The dolphin suit enables more complex response to dolphin body language, as mutual mimicry and playfulness are primary means of dolphin communication. The first time Jan Doak wore the dolphin suit in meeting common dolphins, one individual bonded with her for over four hours, a rare response from this shy species.

The Doaks have found a number of friendly gestures to be successful in communicating intentions to dolphins and engaging them in gamesplay. These include mimicry of dolphin swimming patterns, showing feelings and spontaneous behaviour, responding to their signature whistles by talking back through snorkels, making eye contact, and responding to their gestures.

Some of the many ways in which dolphins make signal gestures to humans are leaping at significant moments, deliberately splashing people on boats after first making close eye contact, vocalising or whistling through the blowhole after people have made communicative calls or whistles, defaecation and touching. Examples of gamesplay are playing with strands of seaweed, bubble gulps, and sexual behaviour.

Among a group of dolphins around the bows of a boat, certain individuals will be most attentive and keep returning again and again. Doak is quite sure that dolphins have varied personalities or behavioural traits, despite the uniformity of their bodies. It is important to observe and respond appropriately to these individuals, recognising them by their distinctive fin markings, body scars and other distinguishing features.

As part of Project Interlock, Doak began publishing newsletters, in which he would write of his own experiences and invite others with similar interests to record theirs. The response was staggering – reports of encounters with dolphins now range across species and latitudes.

Doak now has over 30 written accounts of dolphins living in close proximity to humans. The most complex and prolonged human/dolphin associations have been with bottlenose dolphins, but Doak thinks that they are by no means limited to this species. He invites everyone on this journey of discovery into the potential for interspecies communication.

# The Evolutionary Journey of Dolphins

Five hundred million years ago there was life in the sea but none on the land. Then some sea creatures developed lungs and the ability to breathe air and they moved out of the ocean on to dry terrain. Land mammals evolved, with a backbone and warm blood, carrying their young in their bodies and suckling them with milk after birth. As the ages passed, a few land mammals, the distant ancestors of today's whales and dolphins went back to the sea, and gradually changed shape as they adapted to an underwater environment. The earliest cetaceans are thought to have been related to primitive ungulates or hoofed mammals, who returned to the sea some 50 million years ago. Cetaceans today still carry in their bodies some of the physical traits of their land-dwelling ancestors. The structure of a dolphin flipper resembles the bone structure of an arm and hand with fingers, and a dolphin still has pelvic bones and remains of hipbones that once held limbs.

First entering shallow equatorial seas, then estuaries and coastal oceans, the prehistoric cetaceans spread through the seas of the world. At each stage of their return to the sea, they became specialised to their particular habitat, some going back into freshwater rivers, others frequenting shallow coastal waters or the deep oceans. Eventually, 25–30 million years ago, two great groups of whales and dolphins emerged: the baleen whales (which filter-feed and lack teeth) and the toothed whales. All dolphins and porpoises belong to the latter group.

## Fossil Records Trace Extinct Species *by Ewan Fordyce*

Dolphin history is revealed by fossils from ancient marine sediments now exposed on land. Most work on fossil dolphins has been done in the Northern Hemisphere, and little is yet known about the South.

Fossil dolphins – small toothed cetaceans – encompass the ancestors of modern groups and other groups now extinct, and species are identified wholly on bones, most reliably on skulls, jaws, and earbones. Three living dolphin groups have a record that extends back to about the late Miocene period some 11 million years ago. These are the true dolphins (family Delphinidae), porpoises (family Phocoenidae), and narwhals and their relatives (family Monodontidae). Records show that dolphins have repeatedly colonised fresh waters, and that the living river dolphins, although unified by habit, are not all closely related to one another.

The ancestry of most dolphins is not clear (although this is a very active field of research at present), and with further work the records of most groups probably will be extended further back in time. Few fossils from the critical Oligocene epoch (24–36 million years) are known, and even fewer are described. Back beyond the Oligocene there is evidence only of archaeocetes, the rather large ancestral toothed whales that apparently gave rise to both the Odontoceti and Mysticeti.

It seems that fossil dolphins, like living odontocetes, used echolocation to navigate and find prey. Even the earliest dolphins, such as late Oligocene kentriodontids (about 24 million years ago), have the skull and earbone structures thought to indicate their use of echolocation. There is clear evidence, in fossil skulls, of bony sinuses identical with those used by living dolphins to produce high frequency sound. The use of high frequency sound should have led to the development of sound-processing parts of the brain, although it is not clear whether any extinct form had as large a brain cavity as seen in some modern delphinids.

Dolphins are probably as diverse now in terms of numbers of species, as at any time for which we have a good fossil record. However, today most of the species belong to one family, Delphinidae, with a modest contribution from Phocoenidae. In contrast, the families which contain the different living river dolphins seem to have been more diverse in the past, and were also more widely dispersed. Why these groups became less diverse, and why other dolphins disappeared completely, is unclear. Examples of extinct families include the shark-toothed dolphins (Squalodontidae), and groups such as the Squalodelphidae, Acrodelphidae, and Albireonidae. These might be seen as representing early "experiments" in dolphin lifestyles that did not persist, despite the abundance of the species involved. Squalodontids were mostly medium to large animals (perhaps 3–6 metres or 10-20 feet) characterised by shark-like teeth. Different species differed in number and size of teeth and proportions of the jaws. Acrodelphids, uncertainly related to the living Ganges River dolphin, included some species with an exceptionally long, narrow, flattened beak. Judging from skull form, these now-extinct groups were probably reasonably efficient feeders, which poses questions about the causes of their extinction.

Climate change was probably important in both extinction and evolution of dolphins. Climate can affect marine organisms directly, through temperature intolerance, and indirectly, through affecting food resources. Climatic changes may be short term, like El Nino, or long term, like global cooling or warming over millennia. Climatic changes do affect oceanic food resources, so in the past such changes could have provided new evolutionary opportunities or forced extinction through loss of food. For example, the earth cooled with the development in the Oligocene (perhaps 30–35 million years ago) of the Southern Ocean and Circum-Antarctic Current, and at this time early odontocetes and mysticetes appeared. Conversely, global climates started to cool late in the Miocene, at about which time some formerly common dolphin families disappeared.

Competition between different groups of dolphins might have led to extinctions in some groups, but there is no direct evidence. It is plausible that the diverse delphinids of modern oceans are more efficient feeders which merely outcompeted other small dolphins.

There is no clear evidence that any group of dolphins became extinct because of competition from animals other than cetaceans. Fossil dolphin bones occasionally carry tooth gouges, traces of attack by sharks and other predators. Ancient dolphins might have competed for resources with seals, giant penguins, and other sea birds.

Extinction, like evolution, is a natural process that occurs in response to changing opportunities. Humans should not further tip the balance against living dolphins. The natural world is tough enough without interference.

# 3.  AN EQUAL INTELLIGENCE IN THE SEA?

Dolphins have an impressive ability to imitate and learn, often apparently for the sheer pleasure of doing so. This, together with their displays of co-operative and seemingly altruistic behaviour, and their large brain size, has inspired many studies into the nature of cetacean intelligence. The fascinating question raised is, are dolphins conscious, aware, and conceptualising creatures, with whom we can communicate and from whom we have much to learn?

All the small whales and dolphins have very large brains, roughly equivalent to the size of a human brain, although variation among species is considerable, even among species of similar body weight. However brain size alone is not an absolute indication of intelligence – elephants, for example, have brains four times the size of our own. The ratio of brain weight to spinal cord weight is considered a better measurement of complexity and intelligence.

In fishes, the brain weighs less than the spinal cord; in the horse the ratio is about 2.5 to 1; in the cat 5 to 1; in apes about 8 to 1; and in humans about 50 to 1. The bottlenose dolphin has an average ratio of 40 to 1, the dusky dolphin about 35 to 1, and Dall's porpoise about 26 to 1, suggesting that dolphins generally show a degree of intelligence comparable with that of humans.

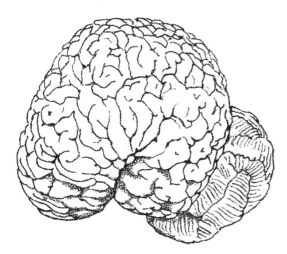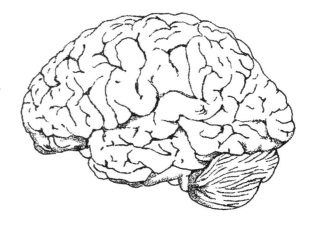

*Comparative size of human brain (right) and that of a bottlenose dolphin (*Tursiops truncatus*). Bottlenosed dolphin brains are more deeply folded than human brains, which increases the surface area of the cerebral cortex – the "thinking" part of the brain. This is considered a measure of certain forms of intelligence.*

Another feature of advanced mammalian brains is the amount of folding in the cerebral cortex, generally considered to be the area responsible for "higher" thoughts and behaviour. One often reads that the human brain shows a greater degree of folding than that of all other mammals, but in fact the brains of some dolphins are more convoluted. The average surface area of the cortex of bottlenose dolphins is half as great again as that of humans. Although the dolphin brain has a large surface area of cortex, it is relatively thin, and the thickness of the cerebral cortex of humans is twice that of dolphins. Nevertheless, the total average volume of the cortex in bottlenose dolphins is just over 80 percent of the average human brain cortex.

## EXPLORING INTERSPECIES COMMUNICATION

Scientific study of whales and dolphins began as far back as the fourth century BC, when the Greek philosopher Aristotle observed and experimented with live animals. His account of the common dolphin, written nearly 2500 years ago, is so thorough that little can be added to it even today. The physical difficulty of working with oceanic animals has limited cetacean study in the past, and much of the information available on whales over the last few centuries has, ironically, come from the whaling industry.

When in the 1950s attempts to keep dolphins in captivity finally succeeded and the entertainment value of dolphins was suddenly realised, the demand for dolphin shows led to a rapid escalation of the numbers of dolphins captured alive. Dolphin studies then focussed on dolphins in captivity, and trainers and researchers alike were amazed at the speed with which dolphins could learn. Dolphins were often cruelly maimed or killed during such research, but, thankfully, today's studies tend to focus on animals in the wild, and mostly aim to be as non-intrusive as possible. Roger Payne made a breakthrough in studying cetaceans in their natural environment, with aerial photography and new techniques of measuring and recording. He was able to provide information on age, sex, and growth of whales for the first time without killing, touching, marking, or molesting a single animal.

What is becoming increasingly evident is how much we have to learn from dolphins – and how much they may have to teach us. There are numerous accounts from researchers or trainers who start their contact with dolphins thinking they will teach a dolphin how to communicate with humans, and end up wondering if in fact the dolphin has been trying to teach us a thing or two about communicating with them.Numerous formal studies have been made to determine the intelligence of the bottlenose dolphin, according to its performance in tests on classical learning, discrimination, and problem solving. The results suggest that its intelligence lies somewhere between that of a chimpanzee and a dog. However, as Dr Lyall Watson has pointed out, the conclusions must be suspect because the experiments required the animal to do repetitive and meaningless tasks in isolation – a far cry from the dolphin's natural condition. "Humans, under similar conditions, score considerably less well than pigeons."

Traditionally, we have tended to use dolphins' ability to understand and communicate with us on our terms as a measure of their intelligence. But this is more a measure of the limitations of our own mind. Says Joan McIntyre, president of the Project Jonah organisation for many years: "Try for a moment, if you can, to imagine the imagination of a whale, or the awareness of a dolphin. That we cannot make those leaps of vision is because we are bound to a cultural view which denies their possibility." We need to stop evaluating intelligence purely within the model of our own. Just because dolphins use language in a different way does not mean that they lack high intelligence or cannot communicate. Their brains are as large and as complex as ours, and in fact evolved to this size and complexity several million years earlier than human brains. Having so long regarded our intelligence as supreme, perhaps we should now consider the possibility that other creatures may be equally intelligent and possess a communication system that is beyond our comprehension.

"To enter into the perceptual world of whales and dolphins, you would have to change your primary sense from sight to sound. Your brain would process, synthesise and store sound pictures rather than visual images. Individuals and other creatures would be recognised by the sounds they made, or by the echoes they returned from the sounds you made. Your sense of neighbourhood, or where you are and who you are with, would be sound sense."

*Dr Peter Marshall,*
*US environmentalist and naturalist*

John Lilly, an experimental neurologist, founded the Communication Research Institute in the Virgin Islands to explore the potential of the dolphin's large and complex brain. During the 1960s, he demonstrated that dolphins could produce sounds in air that seemed to be direct and relevant imitations of human speech patterns. In one long experiment a woman and bottlenose dolphin lived together constantly for several months. Lilly believes that humans and dolphins can communicate with each other despite their physical differences, and he has constructed a complex computer system to send translated messages between human and dolphin.

Louis Herman, at the University of Hawaii, has devised a series of new experiments in which dolphins have learned to understand sentences. Using simple tones to represent words, Herman has taught a dolphin called Akeakamai (Lover of Wisdom) to recognise some 40 or 50 verbs and nouns, which can be combined into more than 1000 different sentences. At present, Akeakamai can understand sentences of up to five words, and can understand commands even when hearing them for the first time.

Dolphins interact with each other and with their environment primarily through the use of sound, and their manipulation of sound greatly surpasses the control shown by any human musician or that needed to operate any human device. Their sonar system enables them to communicate with each other, to "see" through echolocation, and they can possibly even stun fish sonically. Dolphin sounds are unintelligible to humans, and cover a larger range of frequencies than we can hear or differentiate. To us, their noises sound just like buzzes, clicks and high-pitched whistling.

The dolphin's melon, a waxy, lens-shaped organ, extends from the blowhole to the beak and contains much fine wax-oil held in suspension by a very fine web-like tissue, which resembles the inside of a pipless, unripe melon. Many bioacoustic experts agree that the echolocation clicks are created by implosive movements of air in the nasal passages, but the exact process of sound production and projection is unknown - possibly, the echolocation waves pass through the melon. The manner in which the dolphin receives the returning echoes is also a mystery, but they are thought to be picked up by all parts of the body, to travel through the bones to the head. A significant proportion of the dolphin's brain is thought to be used in processing the information produced by the echolocation system.

The real significance of these comparisons remains unknown, as do the real workings of the dolphin mind, but it seems that dolphins and porpoises achieved their modern enlarged brains about 15–20 million years ago, whereas the the evolution of the human brain is a phenomenon of the the past few million years at the most. Moreover, dolphins and other cetaceans have evolved in a watery environment, a much better medium than air for the transmission of sound. Sound has therefore become the most important sense for cetaceans. While human evolution has oriented around the use of hand and eye, and developed down a highly visual and linear path, the dolphin mind has been on a very different track – acoustic, non-linear and non-manipulative.

The properties of water and behaviour of sound are quite different to those of air and sight, therefore the dolphin mind has developed quite different processes of perception, communication and behaviour.

The speed of sound in water is roughly four times as great as it is in air. On the other hand, water is not much different for taste and smell, and much worse for vision. Except at its surface, the sea is dark and shadowy, and underwater creatures are thought to rely mainly on black and white pigmentation for their vision. Off shallow coasts, 90 per cent of white light is absorbed at 10 metres (33 feet) depth, and only one per cent of white light penetrates below 40 metres (130 feet). At depths of greater than 430 metres (1400 feet), the sea is pitch black. Sound behaves quite differently to light. It can bend round corners and pass through objects. While vision depends on the presence of light, sound can be used at any time of day or night and at all depths.

A dolphin emits a steady stream of sounds, each lasting only 10–100 milliseconds. These are short pulses of ultrasonic sound (from 0.25 to 220 KHz), produced in the nasal passages and probably focussed through an organ in the forehead, known as the melon, into a narrow stream of clicks and whistles. The sound waves bounce off objects in their path and are reflected back to the dolphin where they are channelled through oil-filled sinuses in the lower jaw to the inner ear. Through this "echolocation" system a dolphin builds up an acoustic picture of its surroundings, and can hunt its prey over a much greater distance than the limits of visibility in the water.

In the area at the front of the skull are connecting sacs which enable the dolphin to cut off one or all of the four high-frequency signals which may be in operation. As no vocal chords as we know them are to be found in the larynx, the sounds emitted probably come from the lips of the larynx.

A dolphin's vocabulary is varied, with a range of whistles, squeaks, squawks, groans, rattles, clicks, and many other sounds. Most cetaceans have developed two kinds of voices – pulsed sounds such as clicks and burst pulses, and unpulsed sounds like whistles and squeaks. The unpulsed sounds seem to relate to times of heightened excitement, such as during feeding, when stranded or in a state of distress or alarm, or between mother and newborn calf. Pulsed sounds like clicks are used for echolocation and navigation; yelps can be a feature of courtship; and other pulsed calls are made during distress and aggressive confrontation. The click noises are high frequency and travel only short distances, so tend to be used by groups in close contact with each other. Unpulsed whistles carry over long distances, which may explain their frequent use among spinner and bottlenose dolphins, who often form large groups, and the absence of these sounds among the less social species. The two main types of voices overlap in both quality and function, and can be used simultaneously.

Dolphins have a remarkable capacity for vocal mimicry, and they learn to imitate sounds very accurately and quickly. In studies in Hawaii

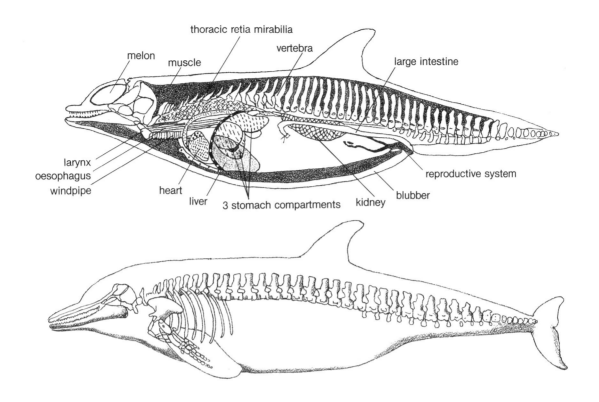

thoracic retia mirabilia
melon
muscle
vertebra
large intestine
larynx
oesophagus
windpipe
heart
liver
3 stomach compartments
kidney
blubber
reproductive system

in 1984, a captive bottlenose dolphin was trained to mimic computer-generated sounds by modifying its whistle. When new computer sounds were made, the dolphin could immediately and with great accuracy copy the previously unheard sounds. Furthermore, the dolphin could relate a sound to an object like a ball or hoop, and thus was able to give vocal labels to these objects. Numerous other experiments have been well documented. Dolphins have been trained to respond to human words, and in Holland a killer whale once spontaneously repeated a human sound. Studies by Louis Herman have established that dolphins are capable of understanding simple auditory and gestural language and can comprehend two- or three-word sentences.

One limitation of these studies, however, is that while they demonstrate the capacities of the dolphin to develop a particular kind of human-derived language ability under the influence of humans, we are still pretty ignorant about the existence of any natural language among dolphin species, although their communication with each other is clearly complex and elaborate.

One clear difference between human and dolphin perception is that because of the ability of sound waves to penetrate objects, the dolphin can listen and "see" through things. A dolphin "listening" to another dolphin can hear inner information with a kind of X-ray vision – body contours can be heard diffusely, teeth and bone reasonably well, and those parts containing air very distinctly. This has considerable significance for the communication of emotional states and personal interaction. It must be virtually impossible for a dolphin to hide its inner emotional state. John Sutphen suggests that with the three sonar channels available to dolphins, cetaceans can see-read-hear into each others' hearts and brains. Telepathic communication, for us still the domain of science fiction or fringe experimentation, may be part of a dolphin's daily life, and may have been so for centuries.

*Upper: Anatomical drawing of a bottlenose dolphin. For simplicity the lungs and intestines, which fill much of chest cavity, have been omitted. Lower: Skeleton of the same dolphin, showing the finger-like bones in the flipper.*

**"Dolphins rely on their oil channels for precise echolocation but sound still impinges on all parts of their bodies with the same high energy and turns every inch into a functional sound receptor. It is not just the surface that is involved either, because sound passes easily through the skin and muscle and bounces back only from bone and air-filled cavities. The internal working of all bodies around him are a normal part of any dolphin's external environment.... When you swim with one he is constantly aware of your health and general well being, of your physiology and the level of your emotional arousal. There is no hiding or lying and no possibility of denial."**
*Dr Lyall Watson,*
Gifts of Unknown Things

In the new project called Project Delphis, the Hawaiian-based environmental organisation Earthtrust is using computer technology to convert dolphin sounds into electrical impulses, so that dolphins can interact with computers via a standard video screen. Unlike John Lilly, who created a computer-generated pidgin language for communication between dolphin and human, Earthtrust's project is establishing an open-ended tool for exploring and demonstrating dolphin intelligence and creativity.

## THE MYSTERIOUS SONG OF THE HUMPBACKS

There have long been stories of mysterious sounds at sea: haunted eerie calls in the night, mermaids singing, sirens luring sailors on to the rocks. Although nineteenth century whalers discovered that many of the strange calls at sea were the voices of whales, only recently have the songs of cetaceans become familiar to the rest of the world. The mysterious and plaintive songs and calls of the humpback whales are now well known, after the efforts of Americans Roger and Katy Payne to record their haunting deep-sea melodies. In these songs, the great variety of cries and moans are repeated over and over in ordered patterns built around a basic unit or syllable that is equivalent to a note in our music. Syllables are grouped in repeating sequences called phrases, and groups of phrases are called themes. About 20 syllables and 6 basic themes have been recognised in the whales' singing, which can continue through day and night with only short pauses for breath. One whale was heard singing non-stop for at least 22 hours. The song of each whale has its own individual signature, but within a season all whales within a region will sing a similar song. These songs are continually changing over the years. Singing is almost entirely confined to breeding grounds, most singers are males, and they mostly sing alone. The songs of the whales carry through the water, over long distances with astonishing clarity, and were heard clearly through the wooden hulls of the old whaling ships in calm weather, giving rise to the belief that the sounds were the songs of mermaids.

Humpback whale songs change throughout the breeding season, as males change their songs in a bid to attract females. Unsuccessful suitors copy the songs of the successful ones, and so the songs change steadily through the breeding season. Researchers have discovered that significant changes in the same songs have been copied by humpbacks on opposite sides of the Atlantic Ocean within 6 days, far faster than a whale could swim the 5000 or so km (3250 miles).

# 4:  A REMARKABLE ADAPTATION TO LIFE UNDER WATER

Dolphins have developed many adaptations to survive and succeed in a marine and, to a lesser extent, freshwater environment. Their bodies are streamlined for maximum efficiency in moving through water, and they have evolved a highly sophisticated sonar system to communicate and receive information through water and over long distances.

## Streamlining and swimming

The external body features like arms, hands, legs, and genitals of the dolphin's land-based ancestors, have either been eliminated or withdrawn inside the dolphin's body to create the most beautifully proportioned and elegant of forms, perfectly streamlined for movement in the water.

The shape and musculature of a dolphin do not alone account for its speed and swimming efficiency, and biologists have long been searching for features of the skin which may explain the mysteries of the dolphin's swimming prowess. It seems that the dolphin has been able to eliminate frictional drag and turbulence when it swims, a feat never achieved by any human-made vessel. A perfectly streamlined form creates no turbulence and only minimal drag, and fluid layers are able to flow smoothly over each other. One of the explanations for the dolphin's superb streamlining seems to be that while they are swimming their skin surface shifts in folds or ripples, caused not by muscular action but as a response to changes in pressure on different parts of the body. This constant changing of shape could be a way of continually inhibiting turbulence.

The dolphin's skin is designed to aid maximum swimming efficiency. Unlike most mammals, a dolphin's skin is hairless, smooth, and thick with no glands. Body heat is retained by a layer of blubber under the skin. Skin cells are shed and replaced rapidly, and whole sheets of skin are often found in pools where dolphins are held in captivity. The outermost skin layer of the bottlenose dolphin is replaced every 2 hours, which is nine times the rate of human skin renewal.

Another feature of dolphin skin which could offset turbulence and accelerate movement is a system of dermal ridges (similar to those that make up our fingerprints) which are found beneath the skin on the back and flanks of most cetaceans, and seem to correspond to the patterns of water flow. The secretion of lubricating oily substances on the skin may also help the dolphin's speed through the water.

Dolphins are incredibly graceful and efficient swimmers. Powering themselves with their tails and using their flippers for steering and balance, they are often seen travelling at speeds greater than 45 km per hour (25 knots), and the fastest species can reach maximum speeds of over 56 km per hour. They'll frequently jump clear out of the water while swimming fast, enabling them to maintain their speed while coming to the surface to breathe. Dolphins are capable of remarkable feats of aquabatics. Walking backwards on their tails and soaring to astonishing heights to nod balls or jump over ropes are common features of public displays.

## Breathing and Diving

Like all mammals, dolphins need air to live, and the first act of life of a newly-born dolphin is to find its way to the surface to breathe. The dolphin has undergone some remarkable adaptations in order to survive a life in which it is under water much of the time.

Cetaceans breathe through a blowhole at the top of their heads, enabling them to surface to take a breath while still swimming. The blowhole itself is the hinged flap of a watertight valve, and through it the dolphin can empty and refill its lungs in the unbelievably short time

Dolphins and whales can store large reserves of oxygen, not only in their large veins and blood sinuses, but also in their muscles. A diving whale may store more than 40 per cent of its oxygen intake in its muscles, far more than a human is capable of. Cetacean muscle is usually very dark because of the presence of the respiratory pigment myoglobin, which acts as an oxygen reservoir.

The condition known as the "bends" is caused by the absorption of nitrogen into the bloodstream from the air in the lungs. As the pressure increases, so does the amount of nitrogen forced into the bloodstream of a SCUBA diver. Unless the pressure is reduced very gradually, the nitrogen can be released from solution as small bubbles, which can lodge in joints, causing severe pain, or in vital blood vessels, causing paralysis or death. At 100 metres (325 feet), a dolphin's lungs are probably completely collapsed - all the air has been forced into the thick-walled windpipe and nasal passages, from where no nitrogen can be absorbed into the blood. As the air in the lungs was at only atmospheric pressure when inhaled, the amount of nitrogen absorbed into the dolphin's bloodstream is insufficient to cause bubbles to form on surfacing.

of one-fifth of a second. Directly below the blowhole are twin valves which separate and direct the incoming air into two streams to supply the two lungs. These valves also serve to trap any water which may accidentally pass the blowhole, and thus prevent it from entering the lungs, which would cause choking or drowning. When a dolphin becomes trapped in a net, it drowns because it is unable to get back to the surface to refill its lungs when the supply of air runs out. Net-caught dolphins frequently have lungs filled with water. Dolphins breathe far less frequently than humans, and compensate by taking deeper breaths and extracting more oxygen from the air they do take in. They can also store more oxygen. Their lungs are not particularly large, despite the fact that a dolphin can hold its breath for five minutes or more, and some species of whales can submerge for up to an hour and survive on a single breath. Efficiency, not size, enables this feat. They fill their lungs to capacity, and change up to 90 per cent of the air with each breath, whereas humans only fill one-eighth of lung volume on an average breath.

Dolphins are superb divers. Many species can dive to depths of 200 metres (650 feet), and several, such as the Pacific variety of bottlenose, and Fraser's dolphins, have been reported to reach 500 metres (1625 feet), in dives lasting over 8 minutes. Some small whales perform even more impressively – pilot whales can go to 600 metres (almost 2000 feet) in a dive lasting 18 minutes, and the beluga can reach 650 metres (more than 2000 feet).

Moreover, cetaceans can dive to these remarkable depths and return rapidly from great deep-sea pressures without suffering from any of the compressed-air conditions like the "bends", which can so easily kill human SCUBA divers. A dolphin dives with its lungs filled, and copes with the crushing effects of pressure at these depths by collapsing its chest as the water pressure compresses the air in its lungs. The collapse is possible because many of the ribs are not joined to the sternum, and those that do join make contact by long flexible cartilages. The ability to collapse their lung air-sacs with increasing depth is probably the dolphin's major protection against the bends.

Like seals and other diving animals, dolphins exhibit bradycardia – the slowing of the rate of heart beat. Bottlenose dolphins have a heart rate of 80–90 beats per minute just after "blowing", slowing within a few seconds to 33–45 beats per minute and remaining at that rate until the next blow. On surfacing, the rate again speeds up, generally remaining at the higher level until the carbon dioxide content of the exhaled air has returned to normal – usually in a few seconds. Through the condensation set up by the intake of cooler air into a warm-blooded animal, a dolphin receives a supply of fresh non-salt water when breathing. Despite the old prints which showed whales spouting water, the blow is simply water condensation. Paradoxically, although surrounded by water, dolphins, like other marine mammals, tend to lose water from their bodies to the sea. They compensate for this by gaining water from their food both through the workings of their powerful kidneys, which extract much of the water from the urine, and by the condensation of water during breathing.

## Feeding

When the ancestral cetaceans returned to the sea, they had to adapt to the much colder temperatures of water, which conducts heat 26 times more efficiently than air. A thick layer of blubber beneath the skin helps insulate cetaceans against temperatures that would quickly kill a human. Humans become unconscious after being submerged for 3 hours in water at 15°C (60°F). Dolphins also have a higher metabolic rate than terrestial mammals of a similar size. The harbour porpoise, for instance, needs to maintain a rate three times that of an equivalent-sized land mammal to keep itself warm in cold waters. The dolphins' high-protein fish or squid diet, with almost no carbohydrate content, also contributes considerably to a high metabolic rate. Those species studied have large thyroid glands and a high level of circulating thyroid hormones.

Much of a dolphin's life revolves around finding and eating food, and it has evolved a highly developed jaw and sonar system to serve its feeding requirements. The toothed whales have a set of teeth which they use to grasp large and quick-moving prey, mainly squid or fish. The number and size of teeth varies greatly among species, and in some of the dolphins and small whales, teeth have become virtually non-functional. The common dolphin has a total of 180 teeth, which it uses to hold the captured meal fast while it is turned around to be swallowed head first. Dolphins that feed mainly on squid usually have fewer teeth and have developed other adaptations to hold on to their slippery-bodied meals. Beaked whales generally have only a single pair of teeth protruding from their lower jaw, and instead of teeth they use a ribbed palate to get a firm grasp on their prey.

The narwhal also has only two teeth, and in the male (and occasionally the female) one of these grows outwards to form a long, impressive, spiralling tusk. This tooth tusk is thought to be used more for jousting matches than to help in feeding, and narwhal tusks brought back to Europe by early ocean adventurers almost certainly inspired the legends of the one-horned unicorn. The narwhal has developed other techniques to capture its food, such as sucking or blowing. Its highly flexible neck enables it to keep watch over a wide area while it is both searching for and chasing prey. In contrast, the dolphins that are equipped with good sets of teeth, and the porpoises, which have 13–28 pairs of spade-shaped teeth in each jaw, have a less flexible neck because their neck vertebrae are fused together.

River dolphins have highly specialised feeding behaviour. Their small eyes and poor eyesight, combined with their often murky environment, means they have to rely on a short-range echolocation system to find food. Their inability to see or echolocate over longer distances undoubtedly contributes to their frequency of net entanglement. They have numerous conical pointed teeth, with 24–60 pairs in each jaw. Although unstreamlined and slow swimming, they are highly manoeuvrable, with a flexible neck. Their long slender beak also assists in capturing their prey. They are solitary creatures, usually feeding on their own, searching for prey on the river bed.

Dolphins feed mainly on schools of prey. Here, there is always more food than any individual would need, and because searching for food as a group is more efficient than searching individually, most dolphins have developed communal and co-operative hunting practices. They travel in large concentrated groups to search for food, particularly when herding shoaling pelagic (open sea) fish. Not only can they cover a much wider area than they could on their own, but their collective experience assists in finding food. While searching for prey, many dolphin species move in tight schools distributed over a large area, using sound to stay in contact and communicate with each other over significant distances. A dolphin school will often divide up into sub-groups while searching for food, which separate and spread out over a wide area of sea, still diving synchronously – evidence that they are probably in some form of acoustic contact.

Echolocation, too, plays an important role in food hunting for dolphins and toothed whales. The sonic pulse systems emitted by toothed whales are directional and most species seem to use them not only to detect food but also to make fine distinctions on the basis of the

The baleen whales (Mysticetes) are huge creatures who sieve from the sea small crustaceans and fish through a curtain of fibrous baleen material hanging from their upper jaw. The toothed whales (Odontocetes) have teeth and eat larger prey such as fish and squid. The baleen whales include most of the larger species known as the Great Whales, but represent only 11 of the 77 cetacean species currently recognised. The toothed whales range in size from the smallest dolphins, 1.3 metres (4.2 feet) long and 30-40 kg (66-68 lb) in weight, to the mature bull sperm whale, 18 metres (58 feet) and 50 tonnes or more. Over half the species of toothed whales are dolphins or the closely related porpoises. Scientists characterise dolphins by their pointed teeth; porpoises have spade-shaped teeth and a different bone structure in the skull. In common use, however, the terms dolphin and porpoise are often interchangeable.

Dolphins need to eat considerable quantities of food. A 120 kg (260 lb) Dall's porpoise, a fast-swimming and deep-diving species, consumed 15 kg (33 lb) of fish daily without increasing its weight while held in captivity in California - equivalent to a human eating 7-10 kg (15-22 lb) of steak in a day. And the dolphins' high-protein diet makes them especially vulnerable to environmental contaminants which become increasingly concentrated as they are passed up the food chain.

Dolphins have an ingenious adaptation to cope with eating under water. On the upper surface of the tongue of many species are small perforations, whose purpose is to stimulate the mucous glands at the base of the tongue as soon as the fish is taken into the mouth. This mucus floods the area at the base of the tongue and the entrance to the gullet, adhering to the walls. As the fish enters the gullet, the mucus clings closely to the skin of the fish as well as the walls of the gullet and it closes behind the disappearing tail, thus preventing any salt water from entering the stomach.

echoes. Most dolphins and small whales travel in groups broader than they are long, which allows them to acoustically scan as large an area as possible. The size of the groups is probably determined by the number of individuals that can be sustained by the size of the school of prey. Where the prey is shoaling fish, the schools of common, spinner and spotted dolphins who feed on them can often number in the hundreds, sometimes even thousands.

Once dolphins locate a school of fish, they spread out, some individuals diving down to the school of prey to herd it to the surface by swimming around and under the fish in an ever-tightening formation. The water surface then acts as an entrapping wall, although individual fish will often be seen flying through the air trying to avoid capture. The dolphins may also make loud sounds and a series of echo-clicks which help to herd the fish and may even stun them. Herding and criss-crossing behaviour has been observed in spotted and spinner dolphins, common dolphins, dusky, white-beaked and bottlenose dolphins and probably also occurs in other species. We are unsure whether the behaviour is truly co-operative, or is organised by certain individuals in the school, but the whistles and considerable vocal activity which often occur among members of feeding groups are undoubtedly communication signals.

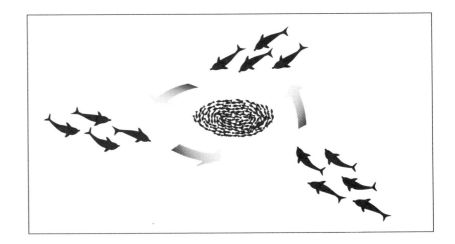

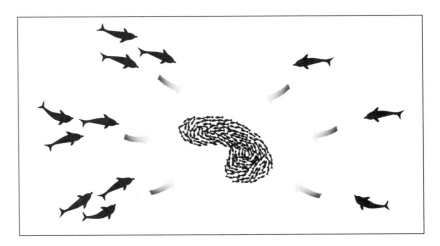

*Food-herding by white-beaked dolphins: Upper: Dolphins converge to bunch the fish together. Lower: A group moves in a U-shaped formation in the direction of a smaller number of individuals, trapping the herded fish.*

# Social behaviour

Earlier this century, studies of the dolphin relied on observations of animals in captivity, and interpretations of social behaviour drawn from these studies are likely to be suspect. In recent years however, scientists have taken a greater interest in the exciting possibilities of observing animals in their natural surroundings. The development of sophisticated photographic techniques and new technologies like DNA-fingerprinting have encouraged an increasing number of cetacean studies in the wild, gathering information not only from a wider range of species, but also in a wider range of contexts and environments. Such information is undoubtedly more valuable than that derived from captivity studies. However, many studies are still done on animals at or just below the surface, where dolphin behaviour is usually affected by the presence of the human observer.

Dolphins are essentially social animals. Most species will form groups at some stage of their life, for feeding, defence, or caring for the young, for example. However, some species, such as the beaked whales and the river dolphins, can be almost solitary. This is easy to understand for the river dolphins, which feed on individual prey on the river bottom, but the habits of beaked whales remain almost a total mystery.

Large groups of dolphins are mixed in age and sex, but smaller groups generally are of three types: a nuclear group, comprising a single adult male and female; a nursery group, with a number of adult females and young; and a bachelor group, with adult and young males. Many communities of small cetaceans have rigid hierarchies of power. Dolphin groups tend to travel in specific formations, exhibiting refined and developed skills in working and co-operating as a group. A navigating formation travels in a wedge shape, with dominant animals and perhaps those with developed sonar skills at the front, and the young of the herd protected in the centre. Other groups will form a parade, and travel in single file on long journeys, or sometimes in open square or hollow circle shapes. For hunting, various formations may be adopted.

Many field studies suggest that the social structure of both inshore and pelagic dolphin species is generally fluid and loose, with probably a promiscuous mating system for most. A core group of individuals does seem to stay in association with each other over extended periods, although there may be some coming and going within that time. Individuals in one group in the morning may have joined another group some 10 kilometres (7 miles) distant by the afternoon or next day. Mothers and calves may remain together for many years, from 3–6 or even 8 years. Segregation by sex and age is relatively common. The age of sexual maturity varies, from only 3 years for the common dolphin to 8 or 9 years for the spotted and the striped dolphins. The larger species tend to reach sexual maturity later, and differences between the sexes are greatest in those species thought to be polygamous. In these, males are much larger than females and take much longer to sexually mature – perhaps the result of the increased time spent in competition with other males to take over a group of females. Many marine mammals (for example, sperm whales, sealions, and elephant seals) show a similar difference in size between mature males and females, especially if the dominant male holds a number of mature females, often known as a "harem."

Behavioural and sound signals seem to be used to communicate sexual interest, and among the toothed whales, with their great acoustic sensitivity, receptivity to sex may be communicated by something which a dolphin can "see" or "hear" with its sonar. Females also indicate their enthusiasm by giving out signals such as changes in the

Group numbers in dolphins may reach into the thousands and oceanic dolphins may gather in numbers exceeding 100,000. Striped dolphins and Dall's porpoise are most often seen in groups of 5-30 and 2-20, respectively, but both have also been observed in numbers of around 300. Most species generally congregate in groups of 6-60 individuals. The size of groups can be difficult to measure, because dolphins apparently travelling separately may in fact be part of a widely spread group in acoustic communication with each other.

Dolphins spend a lot of time enjoying sex and foreplay, and unlike most wild animals, their sexual interest is not determined by being "in season", or the urge to procreate. They are exponents of free love, and generally seem to be promiscuous and ready to make love with everyone, including mothers, fathers, aunts, uncles, and children. Bulls have been observed to mate with as many as 20 females, after much love play, over one and half hours. According to Lyall Watson, this "freedom of sexual expression and emancipation of sex from purely seasonal procreative activity usually indicates a high level of behavioural organisation and development".

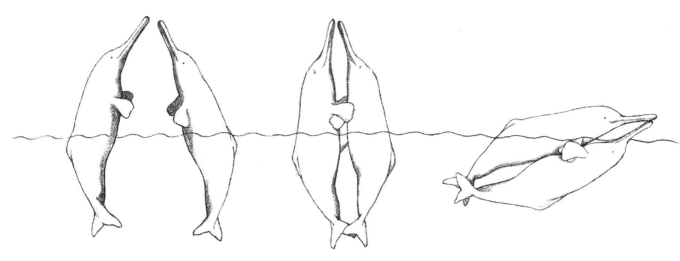

*Courtship of the Ganges River dolphins.*

shape and colour of their genitals, and possibly a discharge of hormones in their faeces or urine. Courtship may take various forms including chases, simultaneous surfacing, breaching, and flipper contact, and sound is almost certainly used to communicate identity and emotion. Harbour porpoises and bottlenose dolphins both make pulsed yelps during courtship. Before mating, pairs may join belly to belly either in an upright position, or with the female lying motionless belly-upwards just beneath the surface. In the latter position the female swims beneath the male, but usually the pair swims with the male gliding beneath the female. Such behaviour may be practised by animals of any age, and at different times of year, and sometimes between the same sex, but does not always lead to mating.

All species of whale and dolphin usually produce a single young. Although female cetaceans do have paired mammary glands, twins have been recorded only very rarely, and even then one or both have died. Gestation normally lasts 10–12 months, but is 15 or 16 months in certain species (usually those for which squid are important prey). The young are suckled usually for 18–20 months, 24 months at most. Some solid food will be taken on average from 6 months of age. The mother's milk is very rich, with a 40 per cent fat content (the fat content in human milk is only 2 per cent). Because of the long gestation and lactation periods, the interval between calving is usually at least two or three years.

A dolphin calf is born tail-first with open eyes, alert senses and enough muscular co-ordination to follow its mother immediately. At birth the mother will help her calf to the surface to gain its first breath, taking about 10 seconds to do so. The mother may be assisted by others (usually non-pregnant females) who often help take the calf to the surface for air. These "aunts" may also help the mother if she is in difficulty, supporting her underneath her body and swimming with her. Young may be carried on the snout of the mother if they are in distress (or stillborn), a behaviour that is also sometimes extended to humans in distress. An attending female has been seen to bite through the umbilical cord of a captive dusky dolphin during the birth of her young, but usually the mother does this herself. Aunts continue to show great interest in the calf after birth, helping to protect it and sometimes "babysitting" the calf. In most cetacean groups, if mother/calf pairs come together, with or without aunts, to form nursery groups, they are segregated from males, who play no part in parental care. Throughout its early life, the calf stays close to its mother, positioning itself above

**The lifespan of cetaceans varies among species, the larger species generally living longer. Examples of average lifespans are 20 years for the common, bottlenose, and Ganges River dolphins, and 25 years for the narwhal. Maximum lifespans may be much greater, some narwhal and spotted dolphin living to 40-50 years, and the Baird's beaked whale possibly to the ripe old age of 70 years.**

the midline and forward of her dorsal fin. During swimming the young may press its flipper against her side and thus be helped to move with her.

As the calf grows older the bond with the mother weakens, although it may last 2 or 3 years. Interactions with other young increase, and similar-aged individuals will form into groups, either of the same or of mixed sex.

## Protection and Aggression

Cetaceans have few predators other than man. Sharks, killer whales, and false killer whales are believed to present some threat to dolphins – scar marks thought to have been caused by shark attack have been observed. However dolphins and toothed whales commonly rake each other with their teeth, as dominant animals show aggression towards subordinates (usually younger males) and in competition for females, and this may also be a cause of scarring.

The common response to predator attack appears to be for the cetaceans to flee, often silently, having first formed a tight group if they can. Sometimes aggression will be displayed, and the predator is pursued or attacked. Bottlenose and hump-backed dolphins have been seen chasing off shark predators and even killing them, but packs of killer whales can encircle and trap a school of dolphins with a curtain of sound, before selecting a few hapless victims.

Despite their fearsome reputation, however, killer whales have never been known to attack humans without the provocation of a bullet or harpoon, although boats have occasionally been attacked and sunk.

## Play and Friendship

Dolphins of all ages are frequently seen playing with each other. Young dolphins repeatedly practise aerial leaps and spins, and fin and head slaps. They will ride the surf or the bows of a vessel, constantly passing back and forth and making boisterous leaps. Young dolphins also play with toys such as feathers and stones in long and involved games. Social and sexual behaviour is common with much tactile contact by young animals, who stroke one another with their penis or flippers, and may swim together belly to belly or touching flippers – something similar to holding hands. They do this throughout life, not only in courtship, and the penis probably serves as a tactile as well as sexual organ. This friendly, affectionate behaviour is often extended to humans.

Much attention has been given to the seemingly altruistic behaviour of dolphins, with various authors citing such examples as the way cetaceans will assist or stand by other ill, injured or stranded animals even to the point of their own death. They are always ready to rescue and support sick or injured animals and help them to the surface to breathe, in the same way that mothers and "aunts" will help their young to take their first breath. Dolphins will also come to the defence of each other in fighting off an attacker or threat, and they are ready to extend these forms of rescue to humans in distress.

"If a dolphin can out-manoeuvre or outswim a shark it will do so.... if the dolphins cannot take evasive action for some good reason, such as that a birth is about to take place, they will attack a shark. The females close in on him, led by some old lady dolphin who has obviously had much practice at settling sharks. She will strike a tremendous blow with the end of her beak. Her mouth is tightly shut and the full weight of her body is behind the blow which the shark gets in the liver and can prove fatal. If he survives this and decides to retreat he is allowed to do so, but if he stands his ground he is doomed. The rest of the females will butt him.... until his liver is pulverised."
*Frank Robson, New Zealand whale and dolphin expert*

*Spotted dolphin. "It is with a feeling of surprise and wonder, even of awe, that humans become aware of a great intelligence living in the sea ..." (Frank Robson)* Bob Talbot

**Above**: *A spinner dolphin. The dolphin body is among the most beautifully streamlined and elegant of forms in nature.* Stan Butler/ Earthtrust

**Opposite**: *A spinner dolphin – the species that suffers the most from purse-seine fishing for tuna in the Eastern Tropical Pacific. By 1979, this species had been reduced to about 20 percent of its original population in that area.* Stan Butler/Earthtrust

**Left**: *Common dolphins travelling at speed. As air-breathing mammals, dolphins have to come to the surface regularly, and this makes them vulnerable to human aggression and drowning in fishing nets.* Greenpeace

*A family group of spotted dolphins. Because they have a low reproductive rate, dolphin populations can be endangered by even small losses of their numbers.* Bob Talbot

*Above*: Dolphins driven ashore and killed at Tatsunoshima Island, near Iki in southwestern Japan. Local fishermen claimed that dolphins like these were stealing fish and threatening the fishing industry – so they herded them up and massacred them.  Susie Cate

*Right*: Conservationist Susie Cate and her son Banyon with slaughtered dolphins at Tatsunoshima Island, near Iki, Japan. Over 6000 dolphins and small whales were deliberately herded into shore and killed in this area between 1976-1982. Most of them were ground up to make fertiliser. Dexter Cate

**Above**: *Dead striped dolphins killed in the Japanese drive fishery are lined up on the dock at Futo Harbour, before despatch to local fish markets.* Earthtrust

**Left**: *Dusky dolphins are the prime target of directed kills in Peru, where around 10,000 dolphins and porpoises are hunted and killed each year for food. There are no reliable figures on dolphin abundance around Peru – no-one knows how endangered local populations are.* Koen van Waerebeek

*Orcas (killer whales) are the most sought-after species for display, but most die during or shortly after capture.* Steve Dawson

# PART TWO

Dolphins and their closely related cousins, the porpoises and small whales, show many of the attributes of intelligence and social awareness which humans have recognised in the great whales. Yet while there has been a concerted worldwide effort to save the larger cetaceans from agonising death by human hands, the small cetaceans have in recent years been dying in record numbers.

# 5: THE SAD STORY OF THE RIVER DOLPHINS

The dolphins that live in the large, silty, turbid rivers of Asia and South America are strange, almost mythical creatures with long sensitive beaks, small near-blind eyes, and broad short flippers. They show features once considered primitive, but many scientists now consider them to be highly specialised.

Their story is one of the saddest, as two species, the Indus River dolphin and the Yangtze River dolphin (baiji), are on the edge of extinction, and their continued survival seems unlikely. The survival of the other species of river dolphin is also precarious and to a certain extent unknown, as accurate figures on population numbers are lacking.

No one knows whether river dolphins were once more abundant or whether their numbers have always been low because of their restrictive and specialised habitat. But they are now undoubtedly the most endangered of the dolphin species, largely because their small and isolated populations are particularly vulnerable to the industrialisation which has occurred throughout much of their range in the past few decades. Besides the destruction of their habitat caused by dam building, silt and pollutant discharges into rivers, and the effects of boat traffic, the dolphins have also had to contend with accidental capture in fisheries, directed hunts for food and other uses, and even capture for display in overseas aquaria.

## INDUS RIVER DOLPHIN

The Indus River dolphin is found only in the Indus River and its tributaries in Pakistan, and was once widespread throughout the 3200-kilometre (2000-mile) river system. Only about 600 dolphins remain, however, and the species is verging on extinction. The Indus River dolphin is a small, essentially blind creature, which swims on its side, hunting for fish by echolocation. It has been traditionally hunted for food and as a source of medicinal oil, and has in recent years been accidentally captured in fishing nets. The dolphin is practically extinct in the Punjab, where only 60 to 70 are reported to survive in the thousands of kilometres of river which were until recent times the home of many more animals. The decline in dolphin numbers in the Punjab is probably largely due to the activities of the local *dagori*, or dolphin catchers. Others die from entanglement in fishing nets.

The severest human impact on this rare creature, however, has been

Most river dolphins are almost blind. They have an extraordinarily sensitive echolocation system, and their huge foreheads enclose a large brain and sound organ which enable them to navigate and detect prey in conditions of zero visibility. During tropical rainy seasons when rivers flood and spread muddy waters over the land, the Amazon River dolphin ranges miles from the river bed seeking fish. Unlike oceanic dolphins, they have articulated vertebrae similar to those of land mammals, which enable them to manoeuvre through tree trunks and roots in flooded forests. They can travel easily in silty water only a metre or so deep, and as the waters recede they can remember the way back to the river bed along deep channels.

the loss of its habitat. During the 1960s and early 1970s, a series of dams was built along the river as part of a massive irrigation system. Six barrages on the Indus itself, and more in the river's tributaries, have created impassable barriers, preventing seasonal migrations and separating and isolating different populations. The dams also render the animals easy prey for hunters and trap them when the water is drained for irrigation.

In 1972 the Government of Sind Province declared the river dolphin protected by law and prohibited its killing and trapping. Several years later, after a recommendation from the World Wildlife Fund, the Government established part of the Indus river in the Sind Province as a dolphin reserve, where 500 of the 600 remaining dolphins are reasonably well protected. The dolphin received further protection in 1975, when the District Magistrate of Sukkur made trapping or killing of dolphins illegal under a Criminal Procedure Code, which was given extensive publicity by drums, through radio and newspapers, and by placing posters in key locations. As a result of these measures, the river dolphin population now appears to be stabilising and even increasing, but the dolphin is still extremely vulnerable and needs continued surveillance at both national and international levels.

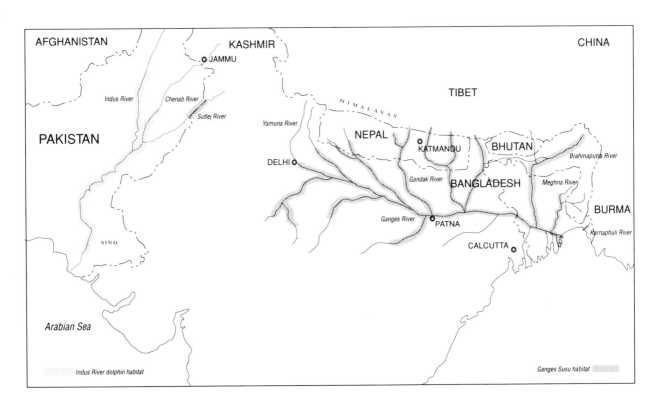

*Map of the Indus and Ganges River catchments, showing the known distribution of Indus River dolphins and Ganges susu.*

As often happens with highly endangered species, this dolphin has been much sought after as a rare specimen for overseas aquaria, and has been captured for display in the US and Switzerland.

## GANGES RIVER DOLPHIN (Ganges susu)

The Ganges susu, closely related to the Indus River dolphin, is a more abundant species found in the Ganges, Brahmaputra, and Meghna river systems, from the estuaries in Bangladesh and Bengal, up to Nepal and the Himalayas. No complete census of dolphins has ever been carried out in India, although the total population is generally assumed to be between 4000 and 5000. The dolphin is under threat from various quarters.

In both India and Nepal, Ganges susu are hunted and killed for their oil. Indian fishermen use dolphin oil to lure catfish into their nets, and in Nepal, dolphins are netted by fishermen and marketed for their oil, which is used as a remedy for a wide range of diseases.

As with the Indus River dolphin, the construction of dams has seriously affected the Ganges susu, both through draw-down of rivers and loss of habitat. The changes in water flows inevitably associated with dams have enormous impacts on the ecology of any dammed river. The lakes created behind the barriers often become de-oxygenated through rotting submerged vegetation. The populations of invertebrates, plankton, and fish change, and top predators such as dolphins may find their traditional prey disappearing altogether.

In Nepal, dolphin habitat has traditionally been in deep clear water with swift currents, but hydro-electric development is occurring in many of the susu's favourite remaining areas. Construction of hydro-electric dams not only removes the opportunity for adjacent populations to interbreed, it also utterly changes the characteristics of the river, with siltation and often stagnation occurring upstream of the barrier.

## THE YANGTZE RIVER DOLPHIN (baiji)

Rivalling the Indus River dolphin for the dubious distinction of most endangered dolphin, is the baiji or Chinese river dolphin, a little-known species found only in the Yangtze River. Once found throughout the Yangtze, as well as the adjacent Futon River, the baiji, 2.5 metres (8 feet) long, is now reduced to a handful of sub-groups. Its total population is thought to be no greater than 200–300, scattered along about 1400 km (875 miles) of the Yangtze's lower and central sections.

About 350 million people live in the Yangtze valley, and its thousands of kilometres of waterways are essential to commerce, industry, and

*Distribution of Yangtze River dolphins (baiji), China.*

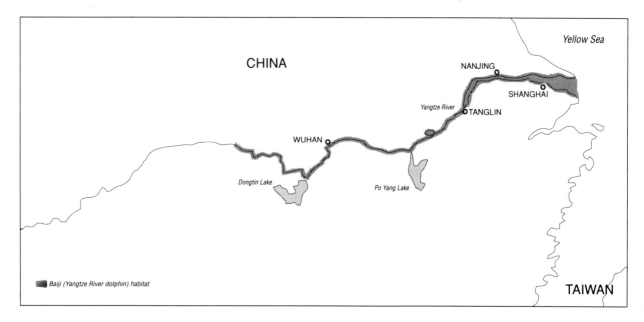

In an attempt to rescue the baiji from extinction, a joint US-Chinese research team is establishing reserves. Scientists from Nanjing Normal University are building display tanks and a semi-natural reserve in the form of a 1.5-km (1-mile) channel between two islands in the river at Tongling. Further upstream, at Shi Shou, the Wuhan Institute plans to adapt a 20-km (12-mile) old oxbow in the river to become a reserve. Even with supplementary feeding, only a few dolphins can be kept alive in such small reserves, which may not be enough to maintain an adequate gene pool. Even here, their future remains in the balance. The announcement in late 1992 that the Chinese Government will proceed with the enormous Three Gorges hydroelectric dam will surely destroy the remaining baiji habitat and seal its fate in the wild.

fishing. The Yangtze River valley supplies 40–70 per cent of China's annual grain harvests, and is home to nearly three-quarters of the country's heavy industry. The river system serves simultaneously as a commercial waterway, a source of huge volumes of water for industry, and a sink for the wastes and debris of modern society, as well as a source of food for the human population and a livelihood for tens of thousands of fisherfolk. Increasing volumes of boat traffic along the river, pollution, industrial activities along the river bank, siltation, and incidental mortalities from fishing all contribute to the baiji's decline.

Like China's famous panda, the baiji is a fully protected species, recognised as part of China's natural heritage, and the Chinese government has taken several steps to improve the prospects for the animal's continued survival into the twenty-first century. Education programmes have been established to inform river-based communities about the plight of the baiji. Laws have been passed to restrict the use of the "rolling hook" fishing method, in which groups of large unbaited hooks are placed on the river bed, with the intention of impaling large catfish. Unfortunately, river dolphins and catfish inhabit the same river, and between 1950 and 1980, about half the 100 or so baiji found dead had died from swallowing or being snagged by fish hooks. Even in areas where the use of nylon set-nets and "rolling hooks" are officially prohibited, these practices are still in use and are responsible for many dolphin deaths each year. Others die from collisions with vessels travelling up and down the river, and from explosions carried out during river bank construction.

The baiji, like the Indus River dolphin, is classified as among the most endangered cetacean species by IUCN. Its survival in the wild far into the next century is unlikely.

## AMAZON RIVER DOLPHIN (boto)

The boto (also often spelt boutu) is found throughout the Amazon and Orinoco river systems, which flow through Peru, Brazil, Ecuador, Guyana, Venezuela, and Colombia, including tributaries upstream in Bolivia. Pink in colour, the boto may be up to 2.75 metres (9 feet) in length. It feeds on a wide variety of fish – 43 different species are known to be taken as prey.

The boto is credited with many natural and supernatural powers. Some stories tell of botos coming up underneath canoes and taking off with the paddles, leaving a lone canoeist adrift on the river, while at other times the dolphin is said to have saved the lives of people from a capsized boat. The boto is certainly credited with keeping away the flesh-eating piranha fish. They are also believed to come ashore during fiestas and dance with village girls, and they are held responsible for many a fatherless child.

The boto is protected by law in Bolivia as well as Brazil. Human pressures on the Amazon, however, are intense, and the dolphin's habitat is being rapidly developed and degraded. There are no reliable estimates of the past or present size of its populations, or of the rates of losses, although fishing is clearly a major cause of accidental death. According to two post-graduate researchers who were studying the dolphin in Brazil, Vera da Silva and the late Robin Best, the boto is caught in seine-nets, gill-nets and drift-nets. Apparently, the dolphin has learned to use a partially formed seine-net (which works by encircling a school of fish) to catch fish, while the fishermen wait in the river for the arrival of a large school. In some areas, the dolphins may actually assist the fishermen by herding up the fish. Perhaps for this reason, traditional fishermen generally try to release alive any captured dolphins, but if they are inside the net when it is closed, they may become entangled or trapped and drown.

Large-scale use of set-nets in the Amazon is recent, and has come about because of the worldwide availability of cheap monofilament nylon nets. Although the boto is a powerful animal, and can sometimes tear its way out of nets, more often it becomes entangled and drowns. The boto has also reportedly become adept at stealing fish from this type of net, and may cause considerable damage to the fishing gear in the process.

According to Best and da Silva, the degree of hostility from commercial fishermen towards the boto is unquestionably growing. In the past this has been countered by the numerous superstitions of the indigenous peoples towards the river dolphins, but as the economic pressures of the commercial fishery become greater, these superstitions are likely to become less respected, especially by the younger fishermen.

Development pressures in the Amazon basin, such as the construction of hydro-electric dams, deforestation, and commercial fishing, have brought a flood of new settlers to the area. Many of them are reportedly gun-happy, and have taken to firing shots at the river dolphins. The meat is not eaten and has no market value, but the dried eyes and the sexual organs of the boto are often sold as amulets to increase one's attractiveness to the opposite sex, or to increase the bearer's sexual powers. Eyeballs are sold openly in markets and tourist shops in Rio de Janeiro and other major cities. Other dolphin products are also in demand in Brazil, especially dolphin oil, which is a favourite lure for fish.

Although the populations and the status of the boto are not known, probably numbers are declining. Fortunately, a recommendation made by the Food and Agriculture Organisation (FAO) of the United Nations in its 1960 Report on the Fisheries of the Amazon Region has not been followed, or the situation would be worse still. The FAO report, written at a time of negligible ecological awareness in fisheries management, suggested that populations of dolphins and fish-eating birds should be reduced to raise the fisheries potential of the region.

Like the Indus River dolphin, boto are also sought after by wealthy institutions in developed countries. A steady number of dolphins are captured alive in Venezuela, Colombia, Peru, and Brazil for aquarium display in the US and Japan. Seventy boto have been captured for display in aquaria in the US since 1956. By 1986, only one captured animal remained alive.


# TUCUXI

Also found in the Amazon basin is the tucuxi (it is a member of the hump-backed dolphin family). Although not closely related to other river dolphins, the tucuxi is included here because it shares a similar habitat. The tucuxi is one of the few dolphins to be found in both fresh and salt waters. Its range extends from Colombia, all along the eastern coast of South America in shallow coastal waters, to around Santos in Brazil, and throughout the Amazon River and the lower parts of its tributaries. There are no population estimates, but the tucuxi is currently listed as highly endangered.

The distribution of the boto and tucuxi show considerable overlap, and according to da Silva and Best, both are the victims of accidental death from entanglement in fixed nylon gill-nets. The tucuxi is, however only half the length of the boto, and is thus less able to break out of gill-nets when captured. Although fixed gill-nets may drown more tucuxi, they generally avoid shallow inshore areas, and are therefore rarely caught in the beach seines which are such a hazard for the boto. But drift gill-nets (which are not fixed) present a much greater entanglement hazard for the tucuxi, since they are used in the deep main river channels rarely frequented by the boto.

Although the ranges of the two dolphins correspond geographically, the feeding ecology of the two species is more distinct. The tucuxi preys on some 28 fish species, but only 13 of these are also taken by the boto. Analysis of the frequency of occurrence and the biomass of these fish suggests little competition for food between the two species.

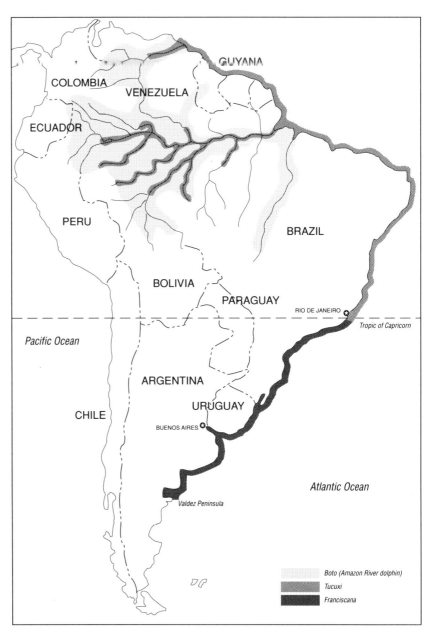

*Distribution of boto, tucuxi and franciscana dolphins, South America.*

Legend:
Boto (Amazon River dolphin)
Tucuxi
Franciscana

Incidental catches in gill-nets are widespread, and the tucuxi is also harpooned in many places along the central and northern coasts of Brazil. They are used for shark bait and for human consumption, and the sexual organs are sought as love charms or amulets.

## LA PLATA RIVER DOLPHIN (franciscana)

The franciscana may be the closest living relative of the baiji. It is one of the smallest cetaceans – adults may be less than 1.3 metres (4.2 feet) long and weigh less than 30 kg (66 lb). It inhabits the Atlantic coast of South America, from the Valdez Peninsula in Argentina to the Tropic of Capricorn in Brazil.

The greatest human impact has been in Uruguay, where 600–2000 franciscanas have been drowning annually in a gill-net fishery for sharks in recent years. Several hundred more are thought to die each year in gill-net fisheries in northern Argentina, and at least 250 were reported incidentally taken in Brazilian fisheries in 1983. There is no reliable estimate of abundance for the franciscana, although the incidental gill-net kill of tens of thousands of dolphins over the last 30 years has undoubtedly significantly reduced the total population. The number of interbreeding populations is unknown, as are chances for long-term survival.

## WHAT HOPE FOR THE RIVER DOLPHINS?

As the terrible inevitability of extinction looms ever closer for the baiji and Indus River dolphin, the international community is belatedly responding to the conservation challenge. The International Union for the Conservation of Nature (IUCN) has developed a 5-year (1988–1992) Action Plan, which features the preservation of the river dolphins as one of its major objectives. The IUCN is seeking funds for several vital programmes aimed at safeguarding these rare and fascinating creatures.

Among these programmes are:
- Baseline studies for a proposed baiji reserve at Shi Shou. The best hope for the beleaguered baiji is the establishment of semi-natural reserve areas where some dolphins can feed and breed without the danger of human interference.
- Establishment of reserves for the Indus River dolphin in the Punjab, where no more than 80 animals are thought to remain.
- Establishment of a Ganges River Dolphin Project, similar to the highly successful Tiger Project which brought together various government agencies, international conservation organisations, and universities in a tightly directed campaign to save remaining tiger habitats and arrest the steady population decline of previous decades. A similar plan to save the river dolphins would need to bring together the major universities and management agencies along the Ganges and Brahmaputra Rivers.
- Surveying the distribution of dolphins and promoting the establishment of dolphin reserves in suitable areas of Bangladesh, India, and Nepal.
- Establishing a dialogue on river dolphin conservation and management between the governments of Brazil, Peru, Venezuela, Colombia, Ecuador, and Bolivia.
- Promoting establishment of river dolphin conservation areas in Brazil.
- Promoting legislation to fully protect river dolphins in Peru, Ecuador, Colombia, and Venezuela, and enforcement of existing laws in other areas of river dolphin habitat.

Whether the headlong rush to develop and industrialise the world's last great wild places can be controlled to ensure the survival of the unique river dolphins will depend on how the respective governments accept their responsibilities to care for and conserve the wonders of natural evolution.

For developing countries with large populations, the problems contributing to the decline in river dolphin numbers are often closely tied to regional and national economies which support millions of people. Yet the current momentum of industrial development is expected to result in the disappearance of no less than 20,000 species of plants and animals over the next decade. As the species which is most obviously shaping the future of planet Earth, humans need to examine the consequences of many current development strategies and urgently find solutions.

"The human standard of living has become the planet's standard of dying.

"How much is really saved by reducing a species to a handful of survivors and banishing them to glorified captivity? What is the real cost of degrading an entire river system to the point that it is no longer capable of supporting its most highly-evolved species?"

*Sam La Budde,*
*US environmental activist*

# 6: THE DELIBERATE KILLING OF DOLPHINS

Tens of thousands of dolphins and small whales throughout the world are still being deliberately and often brutally massacred every year. The stories of "directed kills" are some of the most horrifying of all. Japan, Peru, and the Faroe Islands, Greenland and Arctic regions, and Caribbean countries, are all actively hunting dolphins and small whales for food. Japan shredded a large proportion of the dolphins it hunted and turned them into fertiliser. Turkey greatly reduced dolphin populations in the Black Sea to produce dolphin oil and chicken feed. In Chile, some of the world's most endangered dolphins have been killed for crab bait.

Some of the stories that follow are now history, but the damage to dolphins is irreparable. In most cases the slaughter still continues, driving some species close to extinction. And what we tell here may not even be the whole story. Further reports of deliberate dolphin killings keep coming to light and have yet to be substantiated; the true story may be even worse.

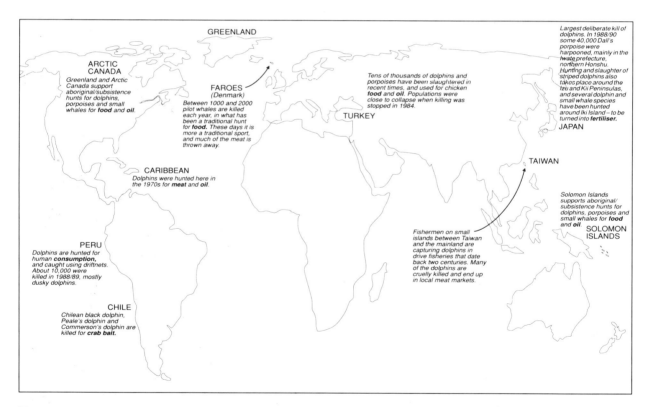

*Main regions of the world where dolphins are still being deliberately killed.*

## KILLING DOLPHINS FOR HUMAN FOOD

### THE JAPANESE
Dolphins have been hunted in Japanese coastal waters since at least the seventeenth century, when drive fisheries were first reported. According to Japanese scientist Masaharu Nishiwaki, the consumption

*Wild dusky dolphin cavorting off the coast of Kaikoura, New Zealand. While a few countries like New Zealand have laws to protect their dolphins, throughout most of the world it is still "open season" on these gentle creatures.* Barbara Todd

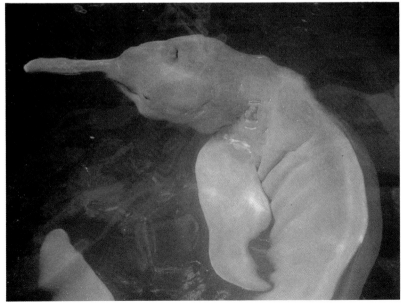

**Above**: *Most dolphin species are highly social, living and travelling in groups. Group sizes vary between species and according to the activity the dolphins are involved in. Here dusky dolphins are travelling in a large group, which may include several hundred animals.* Barbara Todd

**Opposite**: *Amazon River dolphin or boto with Michael Bailey of Earthtrust, in the Pittsburgh Aqua Zoo. Despite frequent attempts to capture and display this species, very few have survived for long in captivity.* Luiz Landgraf/Earthtrust

**Left**: *The Amazon River dolphin or boto is one of the most endangered of all dolphin species, now reduced to only a few thousand in number. Its long beak, tiny eyes, and broad, short flippers, are all adaptations to living in silty river habitats.* Earthtrust

*Above*: Amazon River dolphin body parts on sale in Manaus, Brazil. The dried eyes and sexual organs are believed to increase sexual powers when worn as an amulet. Earthtrust

*Left*: Faroe Islanders in the North Atlantic have for centuries carried out an annual whale hunt called the grynd. Pilot whales, sometimes together with dolphins, are driven ashore with boats and gaffed, speared or knifed to death. Here a gaffed whale is being towed ashore to be killed. Dave Currey/Environmental Investigation Agency

of dolphin was traditionally restricted to poorer people, especially those living in cold coastal and mountainous districts. The blubber was probably considered to be a valuable dietary supplement to help counter the effects of the cold weather.

Now, however, the demand for dolphin meat for the human dinner table is rapidly increasing. Whale meat has traditionally been a popular part of the Japanese diet, but since the International Whaling Commission's moratorium on commercial whaling took effect in 1985, the price of whale meat on the Japanese market has risen dramatically. Now, only the wealthiest can afford to eat it, served in high class restaurants as a great delicacy.

Hunters are cashing in on this shortage and expense of whale meat, and are providing the Japanese market with a more affordable substitute of dolphin flesh. Where an average minke whale would yield between 1000 and 2000 kg (2200-4400 lb) of meat, now some 17–34 dolphins have to die to provide an equivalent amount. Sometimes the dolphin is mixed and sold with whale meat, and called *kurokujira*, or black whale meat, on the Tokyo market.

Many Japanese families today are sitting down to enjoy a meal of dolphin, perhaps eating it raw, or salted and pickled in miso, or dried with seasonings and made into sausage. Other families may be feeding dolphin meat to their dogs. It's a taste that seems to be catching on in Japan, replacing a traditional fancy for whale meat, which is now priced well out of the range of most Japanese pockets. As the demand grows, so does the dolphin kill.

---

## THE DRIVE FISHERIES

The drive fishery is a barbaric practice that often kills entire schools of dolphins. The dolphin flesh is destined for local meat markets, and although Japanese scientists have often appealed to fishermen to release young animals, they are generally ignored since tender infant dolphin meat fetches the highest prices.

The drive fisheries are centred on the Izu and Kii Peninsulas in the southern Honshu region of Japan. The main target is striped dolphin, because it is the easiest to capture. In 1975, a record kill year, approximately 20,000 striped dolphins were killed in the drives. These dolphins are oceanic travellers, with a migration route of thousands of kilometres which takes them past the southern coastline of Japan on both legs of their annual migration. Fishermen of the Kii and Izu Peninsulas therefore have two seasons for hunting dolphins each year.

The city of Ito, on the Izu peninsula, and Taiji, on the Kii peninsula, are the major base ports for the drive fisheries. Dolphin has been a popular food in Ito for many years. The city not only has its own traditional dolphin stew, but also a dish known as *iruka kuroshioboshi*, dried dolphin meat cured to the consistency of leather. It's a popular snack in bars and restaurants.

Members of the Ito Fishermen's Union carry out drives co-operatively. Every time a dolphin school is sighted, the group decides whether to pursue it and attempt the drive. All the fishermen stop fishing to join in the drive. The dolphins have often formed up in groups of up to 3000 when they reach Izu, and they are driven into the narrow inlets of Suruga Bay.

Successful drives often capture the entire group. Catches of as many as 4000 dolphins in a single drive have been reported from the last century, and the record number of animals killed in a single day during the 1970s was 2838.

The average annual catch, mainly of striped dolphins, in the drive fisheries between 1975 and 1986 was 4734. Other species taken in the drives are bottlenose dolphin (average catch 926), Pacific white-sided dolphin (440), and pilot whale (466). Species such as Risso's dolphin and false killer whales are killed in smaller numbers.

# THE DESTRUCTION OF DALL'S PORPOISE

The fast-swimming oceanic Dall's porpoise is a popular food item and has been a favourite target of Japanese harpoons in the province of Iwate (north-eastern Honshu) for many years. The porpoises delight in riding on the bow waves of motor boats, which has frequently proved to be a fatal mistake.

By even a conservative estimate, about 10,000 Dall's porpoise were harpooned each year from 1976 to 1987. However, the director of research on small cetaceans at the National Far Seas Fisheries Research Institute, Dr Toshio Kasuya, believes that the number of dolphins caught, as reported through fishing unions, underestimated the catch by at least 40,000.

Between 1977 and 1981, the season for hunting Dall's porpoise increased from 4 months to 10 months, and in 1987 the number of boats hunting the dolphins and porpoises in the area increased from 200 to 350. By 1988, it had almost doubled again to 600, and boats based on Iwate took over 90 per cent of the total reported Japanese dolphin and porpoise catch.

Kasuya's fears proved to be well founded, and he dropped a bombshell at the 1989 meeting of the IWC's Scientific Committee, when he revealed to the Small Cetaceans Subcommittee the staggering increase in the number of Dall's porpoise killed in the harpoon fishery based on Iwate Prefecture. In 1988, according to Kasuya, over 39,000 Dall's porpoise were killed in the harpoon fishery, not including porpoises that were struck but escaped, possibly mortally wounded. At the same IWC meeting, Kasuya tabled a paper which estimated the abundance of Dall's porpoise in the harpoon fishery area to be no greater than 105,000.

In a single year the unregulated Japanese hunt had killed almost half the estimated local porpoise population.

The Scientific Committee had in previous years expressed concern about the Dall's porpoise harpoon fishery, fearing that even the much smaller annual catch may not have been sustainable, since Japanese scientists had calculated a replacement rate of only about 5000 porpoises each year. However, the scientists' attitudes towards the current catch level were clear. At the 1989 meeting, "the sub-committee concluded that the take was clearly not sustainable and that, depending on the stock composition of the catch, the situation could be even worse than was immediately apparent. For example, the incidental take from squid gill-net fisheries by Taiwan and Korea was unreported and therefore an unknown quantity. The sub-committee said it was a matter of urgency to ensure the catch was reduced to at least the levels of previous years (which themselves had possibly been too high)."

Concerned at the rapid expansion of the hunt, and the declining stocks of small cetaceans around the coastline, the Iwate Prefecture in January 1989 instituted a licensing system, so that for the first time ever, the hunt could be regulated. No new applications for dolphin hunting were accepted, and the number of licensed vessels was reduced from 600 to 540. Only boats under 20 tonnes were permitted, and August and September was declared a closed season. In the face of strident international criticism, the annual quota of porpoises has been reduced, to 22,187 in 1990, and 17,000 in 1991, despite a revised estimate by Japanese scientists, assessing the total exploitable population at 440,000.

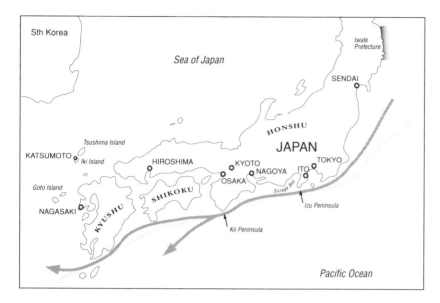

Japanese dolphin hunts are centred on the Izu and Kii Peninsulas in southern Honshu, and the harpoon fishery is centred in the Iwate Prefecture in the northeast. The main target is striped dolphins, whose migration paths (arrowed) take them past the southern and eastern coastlines of Japan every year.

Before 1989, dolphin and porpoise hunting in Japan was unregulated, and from 1981 catches rose steadily so that by 1987 over 21,000 animals were reported taken for human consumption, and the following year officially reported numbers had risen again to over 25,000. In 1989, fishermen received double the price of 2 years earlier. A major attraction of dolphin and porpoise hunting is the low operating costs – all that is needed is a harpoon and fuel for the boat. Some boats are reported to take 500–600 animals during a 3-month season.

As coastal fisheries have become less profitable through overfishing, more fishermen have taken to killing small cetaceans to supplement their incomes. Close to a quarter of a million small cetaceans were killed between 1976 and 1987 in Japan. The dolphins and porpoises are hunted either with hand harpoons or in drive fisheries. Around 2 per cent die in set-nets.

## THE PERUVIANS

In 1985 Peruvian fishermen caught around 10,000 dolphins and porpoises, most of them destined for the fish markets of Peru's capital Lima, making Peru second only to Japan in the consumption of dolphin flesh.

Fish, sea birds, and small cetaceans have long gathered in large numbers to feed in the deep waters off the Peruvian coast, which are among the richest in the world. The Humboldt Current that sweeps up the western side of South America brings an upwelling of nutrient-rich water from the ocean depths. For many years, the Peruvian catch of anchoveta was the largest volume fishery in the world, peaking in 1970 at 12.28 million tonnes. Overfishing, combined with the effects of the cyclical change in currents known as *El Nino* (which can cause widespread collapses in the marine food-web), resulted in the collapse of the anchoveta stocks in 1972, when catches fell to less than one-twentieth of that in the 1970 season.

During the 1970s, many fishermen were forced from the anchoveta fishery and the associated use of purse-seine vessels, and began using smaller boats, setting gill-nets to catch coastal fish species. When these nets also started to fish up cetaceans (mainly Burmeister's porpoise) as an incidental catch, the fishermen discovered a ready market for porpoise meat among lower income groups. By 1975, over 100 tonnes of

When Peru was actively whaling in the 1970s and early 1980s, catching Bryde's whales mainly for the Japanese market, unsuccessful attempts had been made to introduce whale meat to the Peruvian population. Fresh dolphin meat, however, has not met the same opposition, because it has been marketed under the name of *chancho marino*, or 'sea pig'. Furthermore, the public is told that all similarities to dolphins are purely coincidental. According to Koen Van Waerebeek, who has spent many years studying the dolphin hunt, hardly anyone in Peru is aware of the true nature of *chancho marino*. A small proportion of dolphin meat is salted, dried, and sold as long strips known as *muchame*, which was originally introduced by Italian immigrants.

In response to international pressure, the Peruvian Government in 1991 passed a decree prohibiting the deliberate targeting and sale of dolphins. No independent reports have been provided on the effectiveness of these measures, however.

porpoise meat was being sold in Peruvian fish markets, amounting to at least 2000 animals killed each year. Since then, some Peruvian fishermen have specialised in capturing small cetaceans for human consumption. And as the numbers of porpoises have dwindled, they have fished local dolphin populations, in particular dusky dolphins, most of which are caught with small driftnets.

Although the total catch of small cetaceans is only a small proportion of the total landings of fisheries products in Peru, for some ports the landings of dolphins may be very significant. In Cerro Azul in 1984, dolphins comprised almost 19 per cent by weight of the fish and marine products caught for human consumption. Because there are no reliable estimates for the abundance of any of the small cetacean species exploited in Peru, the impact on the dolphin and porpoise populations in the area, or how much longer they can withstand the pressure, cannot be assessed.

A multi-national research team led by Andrew Read of the University of Guelph in Ontario, Canada, and Koen van Waerebeek, University of Ghent, Belgium, monitored the landed catch of dolphins in a number of Peruvian ports during 1986 and 1987, primarily at Pucusana and Cerro Azul. Not only did they monitor landings at the wharf, they also sifted through refuse dumps to find the remains of butchered dolphins, to estimate catches in previous seasons. More than 80 per cent of dolphins are caught in a directed drift-net fishery operating from August to October. Nets, 0.6–1.5 km (0.5–1 mile) long and 7–10 metres (23–33 feet) deep, are usually set at dusk and retrieved in the morning. Catches are better on windy, moonless nights. Dolphins are also harpooned if they approach boats closely enough, and some are also taken incidentally in purse-seines and coastal set-nets.

## FAROE ISLANDS – BUTCHERY AMIDST AFFLUENCE

Participating in a traditional bloody ritual called the *grynd*, that dates back over the centuries, Faroe Islanders each year herd large schools of pilot whales into shallow waters and then, with man and whale alike thrashing in red blood-stained water, the animals are gaffed, speared, or knifed to death. The effect on the whales is tragic – at least 220,000 pilot whales have been killed in these drives since first records were kept in 1709.

To the outsider, the way the whales are killed is nothing short of barbaric. When a herd of whales is sighted, two-way radios carry the news from village to village. The villagers turn out *en masse*, and with motor boats (replacing the row-boats of earlier days) they herd the whales into bays to trap them. The killing can then be a long and slow process, and the animals often have to endure hours trapped in the midst of the bloody massacre of their family, awaiting their own agonising mutilation.

The Faroe Islands, halfway between Scotland and Iceland in the stormy North Atlantic Ocean, were colonised some 1000 years ago by the Vikings. For centuries, their descendants led a harsh and precarious existence, relying heavily on the sea to provide food. The occasional beachings of pilot whales must have provided a welcome source of protein. The Faroese soon developed a drive fishery for pilot whales, and the *grynd* came to be an important social event, an occasion when the whole community would come together to catch their food. The *grynd* continues, but these days the whale meat is no longer needed for food, and islanders are often having to empty last year's whale meat from the freezer to make way for the fresh catch. Large quantities of unused frozen meat and blubber have been found on rubbish dumps after recent drives. Killing has now become more of a sport, or an adherence to an ancient custom. In fact the Faroese are killing more whales than ever. Throughout the 1970s, the average annual catch of

"With repeated strokes they hack into the blubber and flesh of the thrashing animals with 15-cm knives, attempting to cut through the carotid arteries alongside the spine. However finding the artery is very difficult, and often the whales break their own spines by their thrashing.

"Other members of the herd are swimming around in the blood-red sea as this killing continues. It can take several hours to kill an entire whale group which may number several hundred individuals."

*Report of the Faroe Islands pilot whale kills, taken from minutes of the European Parliament, 1989*

pilot whales was 880, but from 1979 to 1984, the average rose to over 2300. In 1987, 1422 whales were killed, and in 1988, the toll rose to 1690 pilot whales. Other species are also victims of the Faroese kills, and in 1988, over 600 other small cetaceans were killed, including 544 Atlantic white-sided dolphins slaughtered in a single drive. White beaked dolphins and three rare and protected northern bottlenosed whales were also killed in this year. In 1989 the reported kill figures were 735 pilot whales and 2 rare bottlenose whales. However, the Faroese government has just committed US$300,000 towards the improvement of two of its main whaling bays – to make whale killing easier.

Until the 1980s the killing of 2000 or so pilot whales each year in the Faroe Islands was considered to be of far less significance than the slaughter of tens of thousands of the much rarer great whale species. After the ban on commercial whaling, however, the IWC is now turning its attention to other species, and international concern is focusing on the Faroes. The Faroe Islands are self-governing, but have been for many years a colony of Denmark, and still rely on the government of the old mother country for international representation. And the IWC has found itself powerless to act to regulate the Faroes hunt because Denmark is claiming that the IWC has no authority over small whales, a view conveniently shared by other countries like Japan and Mexico who hunt or "accidentally" catch dolphins within their exclusive economic fishing zones. The Danish government also claims that however much it may disagree with the *grynd*, it is unable to interfere in the domestic matters of the Faroe Islands.

While the politicians make their excuses, the pilot whales continue to be cruelly slaughtered, and their populations in the North Atlantic grow increasingly scarce. They were caught in large numbers for many years from the north-eastern seaboard of the US and Canada, and the Scottish islands of Orkney and Shetland. Stocks around Newfoundland collapsed through overhunting after over 30,000 whales were killed between 1953 and 1957. Only the Faroese now still hunt them in large numbers.

A resolution of the European Parliament early in 1989 called upon the Faroese to ban the use of the gaff from boats and in water more than a metre deep. This would eliminate the worst cases of cruelty and would substantially reduce the number of whales killed, as only those beached would be gaffed and killed, and the rest could be driven back to sea. Ironically, the best hope for the pilot whales of the North Atlantic is that they are becoming unsafe for humans to eat. High levels of mercury have been reported from Faroese for some years, and the Health Department there has advised islanders to cut down on the amount of whalemeat they eat. More recently, industrial contaminants such as polychlorinated biphenyls (PCBs) have accumulated in the liver and kidneys of pilot whales in quantities which make them unfit for human consumption.

## THE ARCTIC

Some of the world's rarest cetaceans, such as the narwhal, beluga, and harbour porpoise, are still being hunted and killed in the high latitudes of the Arctic. As the commercial whaling industry has declined throughout most of the world, Greenland has been left with one of the highest catches of whales and small cetaceans. Accurate figures for the number of animals caught in these remote freezing areas are hard to collect, but those we do know show the situation to be alarming. In Greenland alone, 1000–3000 harbour porpoises are killed each year, along with 300–600 belugas (white whales) and 400–500 narwhals and some pilot whales.

The most seriously endangered species is the harbour porpoise, whose total Arctic population may be as perilously low as 15,000.

One of the most inhumane aspects of the grynd is the use of a stout metal hook which is driven into the whale's neck, often from a boat. A rope attached to this gaff enables a number of men to drag the whale into shallow water and hold the thrashing animal while others kill it with knives.

Pilot whales are endearing creatures, as anyone who has been involved in their rescue will testify. A middle-sized species of whale, they grow to an average of 7 metres (23 feet) long, and weigh up to 2 tonnes. They are highly social, congregating in groups as large as 500, and the bonding between members of the herd is so strong that if a pilot or lead whale beaches itself, the rest of the herd will often follow, creating a mass stranding.

Beluga populations are also in many places suspected to be at dangerous levels after years of overexploitation. In the mid 1960s annual world catches of beluga were estimated to be around 5000–6000, and 20 years ago in the USSR alone, catches were 3000–4000. Now the USSR catches only a few hundred belugas each year, not only because of enforced catch limits, but because these impressive creatures just are no longer there to be caught in such numbers.

In the freezing barren icelands of the Arctic north, whale and dolphin meat has long been a traditional and important part of the diet for coastal settlements. But many of today's hunts are motivated far more by commercial interests than subsistence needs.

For example, narwhal were traditionally hunted for food by the Inuit Eskimoes of the eastern Arctic region of Canada, who ate the outer layer of meat and skin (*muktuk*) and some of the red meat, and fed the remainder to their sled dogs. In recent years sled dogs have been replaced by snowmobiles, so now the main incentive for the whale hunt is the narwhal's single ivory tusk. This ivory increased in value 180-fold from 1961 to 1982. As the price increased, so did the size of the kill, until in 1977 the Canadian government imposed a quota of 400 narwhals per year.

The recorded catch has been within the quota for many years. But it is unlikely to be an accurate assessment, because shot and mortally wounded whales, unlike harpooned ones, can escape and die without being retrieved and, of course, are not counted against the quota – in fact as many as 1000 narwhals may die each year at the hands of Canadian hunters.

### THE CARIBBEAN

Dolphins and small whales have also been hunted in the Caribbean for many years, especially around the island of St Vincent. They are regarded as a valuable source of meat, and for many years also supplied a US market for oil from the pilot whale melon. In St Vincent, 2912 pilot whales were landed between 1962 and 1974, and these "blackfish", as they are called, were the main quarry of the Vincentian whalers until the introduction of the US Marine Mammals Protection Act in 1972 closed the US market for whale oil. Blackfishing has since gone into decline, but whalers still pursue and kill other small cetaceans, such as killer whales and small spinner dolphins. Between 1972 and 1974 at least 500 dolphins ended up in meat markets in Kingstown, St Vincent.

## OTHER DELIBERATE KILLING OF DOLPHINS

### THE GUNNING DOWN OF DOLPHINS IN THE BLACK SEA

"We have hunted the dolphins for many years. My father hunted them before me and his father before him. Our family has caught dolphins since 1919 and we want to preserve the tradition. We have to kill the dolphins because they eat our fish. But there are fewer dolphins each year and they are more difficult to find."

*Turkish fisherman*

Dolphins have been hunted in the Black Sea since the late nineteenth century, when Russian fishermen sought them for their meat and oil. By the mid 1930s, up to a quarter of a million dolphins were being killed each year by Turkish, Bulgarian, Romanian, and Russian hunters. In 1964, dolphin populations off the USSR's area of the Black Sea collapsed, and by 1966, the USSR, Bulgaria, and Romania had prohibited all dolphin hunting.

Turkey, however, allowed the hunting of dolphins to continue in its waters, and the annual kill continued to increase. In 1969 alone, an estimated 166,000 dolphins were killed by Turkish hunters, most of them shot. No regulations governed the hunt – anyone with a rifle and a boat could kill dolphins without a licence. Almost a million dolphins have been killed over the past 20 years, and the populations of dolphins and porpoises in the Black Sea have been decimated.

As long ago as 1976, the marine resources committee of the FAO believed that "populations of all three dolphin and porpoise species were probably being exploited in the Turkish fishery at levels they would not be able to survive for more than a few years." They urged the closure of the Turkish fishery or a substantial reduction in the catch.

The appeal found no favour with the Turkish government, and the hunt continued unchecked. Little scientific data has ever been released to assess the effect of the killing on the dolphin population, and much of what is known about the hunt has been gathered at great personal risk by non-government organisations.

In 1979, British researcher Suzi Newborn visited the eastern Black Sea area, and confirmed that dolphin hunting was still a popular activity. In 1982, the People's Trust for Endangered Species, a conservation group based in the UK, sent Allan Thornton and photographer David Higgs to document the hunt, and attempt to determine the number of dolphins being killed.

Posing as the authors of a book on fisheries of the world, Thornton and Higgs, accompanied by an interpreter, set off in search of evidence of the continuing carnage. After 3 days, they reached the port of Ordu, where the dolphin hunt was supposedly centred. There they found two boats tied up alongside the wharf, waiting to unload their cargo of dolphin corpses. One vessel was carrying 78 dolphins, the other had 65 aboard – the catch from a 5 day expedition.

Fortunately for the investigators, the fishermen were eager to talk about dolphin hunting. Thornton and Higgs were told that each boat caught about 2000 dolphins each year, travelling up to 180 km (112 miles) offshore to find their quarry. Nevertheless, the rewards were poor. The hunters received on average about US$5 for each dolphin, and the dolphins were all processed at the nearby factory. According to one of the skippers, each hunting trip cost on average over US$130 more than the crew received for the catch – the fishermen were simply carrying on a proud and noble tradition, even though it cost them money.

The reporters then visited the government-owned processing plant at Trabzon, the only factory in Turkey still handling dolphins. Here the carcasses were skinned, the oil extracted from the bodies, and the meat turned into meal to be used as chicken-feed. The manager proved to be very co-operative, and Thornton and Higgs were shown the machines which processed the dolphin meat into round slabs of meal, and a huge open vat of dolphin oil. At the end of the factory tour they saw in a large room more than a thousand dolphins, some piled four or five high. At the far end were hundreds of skinned carcasses. A man with a long knife cut the dolphins' skins and fat from the bodies, by cutting across the dolphin's head, slicing it down the middle, then peeling off the outer layer. As they watched, he skinned a pregnant female and pulled a perfectly formed foetus from its belly.

All these deaths were adding to a stockpile of dolphin oil, which nobody wanted, and meal for poultry food. The hunters were not even breaking even, yet the hunt continued despite the falling catches. Throughout the late 1970s, tens of thousands of dolphins were killed by Turkish hunters each year. In 1980, the catch exceeded 54,000 animals, but in 1981 fell to about 10,000, with harbour porpoises rather than dolphins comprising most of the catch.

The populations of dolphins and porpoises were finally on the verge of total collapse when the Turkish Government suspended the hunt in 1983, and commissioned a report on the populations of dolphins and their effects on fish stocks. Although the report was due in 1987, it has not yet been presented. Turkey is a signatory to the Berne Convention, which prohibits indiscriminate killing of cetaceans.

"…. the weak autumn sunlight spreads across the still waters off the Turkish coast…. The dolphins, engrossed in feeding on an anchovy school, fail to detect the vessels as they make their stealthy approach. "The first shots shatter the morning stillness and three dolphins are struck. The male half jumps from the water, blood pouring from its mouth, before it sinks below the surface. One female is struck in the back, but still attempts to swim away, accompanied by her young calf. A second female is shot behind the eye and swims erratically in half-circles before floating motionless on the surface. The first female is then shot a second time, and as the confused baby attempts to suckle from its dying mother, it too is despatched with a single bullet."

*Allan Thornton,*
*Canadian conservationist*

"Dolphins with bellies slit open thrashed about whistling in distress as their entrails flopped on the concrete. They didn't lose consciousness even as blood gushed from their throats. As we stood there, horrified witnesses, a fishermen deftly severed the heart from a still quivering dolphin, tossing it aside. It landed less than a yard from my feet, still beating."

*Dexter Cate, Hawaiian environmentalist, arrested for releasing 250 netted dolphins at Iki, 6–8 November, 1980.*

Iki fishermen have pursued various quarries over the years. In the 1800s most fishermen were after whales, until their coastal net fishery wiped out local populations. During the early part of this century, the major fishery was for sardines, but local stocks suffered and the industry collapsed in the 1940s. Squid and yellowtail then became the main species fished, but throughout the 1960s and 1970s the pattern was repeated as the yellowtail fishery began to show the familiar signs of overfishing, with catches decreasing despite increasing fishing efforts.

## JAPANESE IKI ISLANDERS TURN DOLPHINS INTO FERTILISER

The small island of Iki, lying off the northern coast of Japan and near to the coast of South Korea, was until very recently the scene of some of the most terrible examples of deliberate dolphin slaughter several times each year. Hundreds of fishing boats drove whole herds of dolphins into bays where they were massacred, most of them destined to become fertiliser. Over 6000 dolphins and small whales were killed on Iki between 1976 and 1982, two thirds of them bottlenose dolphins. Other species that ended up in fertiliser bags included false killer whales (a small whale about 5 metres (16 feet) long and 2 tonnes in weight), Risso's dolphins, and Pacific white-sided dolphins.

The local fishermen alleged that the dolphins were a threat to the local fishing industry, and the Japanese Government was only too ready to support the belief. Reports published by the Japanese Fisheries Agency (a government organisation) between 1968 and 1971 blamed dolphins for damaging fishing gear, stealing hooked fish from fishermen's lines, dispersing fish schools and causing fish to stop feeding. The Agency claimed that the yellowtail angling fishery around Iki suffered in particular.

The sad fact is that although the ostensible reason for the dolphin kills was that dolphins were stealing and eating the commercial fish species, examination of their stomach contents showed that only the false killer whales were actually feeding on yellowtail. To add to the senseless tragedy, the Japanese didn't really know what to do with all the dolphin carcasses once they had killed them. At first most were buried on land, then disposal at sea was tried, weighting the dolphin corpses with cement blocks, a method abandoned in 1979. Live animals were sometimes sent to aquaria, but the demand was limited. A demand for dolphin meat for human consumption has been only a recent trend, but high transport costs from the remote Iki Island made the export of edible dolphin meat uneconomic. Finally a solution was found – large numbers of animals were rapidly disposed of by sending them whole or shredded to a plant which turned them into fertiliser.

As word of the dolphin slaughter at Iki spread, international conservation groups became increasingly concerned, and sent their own investigators to gather first-hand reports. Conservationist Dexter Cate of Hawaii was jailed for 100 days in 1980 when he released several hundred dolphins from the bay into which they had been driven before slaughter. The subsequent outrage from conservationists worldwide spread the gruesome story of Iki Island around the globe and the drives were curtailed after the international condemnation that followed the widespread publicity of the incident.

## THE CRAB BAIT SCANDAL IN CHILE

Chilean fishermen have killed thousands of some of the world's rarest dolphins to chop them up for bait to catch the southern king crab. With the collapse of the Alaskan crab fishery, the local crab industry expanded rapidly, as did the dolphin kills, with an estimated several thousand harpooned or shot each year. The southern king crab seems to prefer dolphin meat to other kinds of flesh also used for bait, such as sea lion, penguin, fur seals and cormorant.

The fishery operates in a remote area at the tip of South America, where the southern king crab frequents the cold waters of Tierra del Fuego. Commercial crabbing began in 1928, but catches increased from 355 tonnes in 1968 to 2680 tonnes in 1984. This huge expansion was the result of increased fishing technology, better boats, and the free market policy adopted by the Pinochet government in Chile in the 1970s to try to tackle its crippling debts. The industry was geared towards maximum use of the resource, short term profits, and foreign dollars, and overseas restaurants were keen to provide markets after the collapse of the Alaskan king crab fishery. Almost all Chilean crab is exported, mainly to the US, West Germany, France, Belgium, Holland, Italy, and Japan.

Despite the large profits made by the industry, only four of the 26 companies involved provided bait to the fishermen, and the amount supplied was grossly inadequate. So the crab fishermen massacred dolphins. Not only were they free, but one dead dolphin could bait over 350 traps.

Although the remoteness of the region makes accurate information hard to come by, in 1979, even before the main expansion of the industry, an estimated 4100 dolphins and porpoises were being killed each year for bait. During the late 1970s, Commerson's dolphin was the most heavily hunted, but recently this species has become less abundant and the crab fishermen turned to Peale's dolphin, dusky dolphin, Chilean black dolphin, and Burmeister's porpoise. A study by US scientist Stephen Leatherwood in 1984 suggested that between 2600 and 3000 black dolphins had been taken for crab bait in only two years.

Dusky dolphins and Burmeister's porpoise are considerably more abundant and wide-ranging than the other three species. Chilean national laws do protect dolphins, but weak and ineffective enforcement meant that until recently no effort was made to regulate the dolphin kills associated with the crab industry. Despite the fact that crab stocks were declining through overfishing, the government buckled to pressure from the fishing industry and actually eliminated a closed season on crabbing in 1983. Recommendations to the contrary made by the Chilean state agency Instituto de Fomento Pesquero (similar to the US NMFS) were ignored.

However, as the story of the crab bait scandal spread, Chile came under increasingly close scrutiny. Environmental groups began efforts to ban the export of Chilean fisheries products to the US market through the provisions of the MMPA. Concerned at the prospect of losing valuable market share, the Chilean Government approved a new fishing law in October 1991 which banned the use of dolphins for crab bait. Additionally, a seven-month closed season was introduced for the stressed crab fishery and fines for illegal activities were greatly increased.

Although the announcement of these new conservation measures has been widely welcomed, fishermen in these remote regions are paying only limited heed to the pronouncements of the Santiago government. The lengthy closed season means that only half the amount of bait is now required each year, but dolphins are reportedly still being taken for bait, albeit in reduced numbers. Due to the low abundance of small cetaceans in the channels of southern Chile, sea lions and penguins have become the main target for illegal crab bait.

To use rare and endangered dolphins for crab bait must be one of the most depressing examples anywhere in the world of commerce brutally overriding humanity. In just a few years, Chilean fishermen have inflicted damage on dolphin stocks which will take decades, if not centuries, to repair. If the situation continues unchallenged, not only will local populations of rare dolphins be wiped out, but the threat of extinction looms not far behind.

Like so many of the problems threatening dolphins all over the world, the Chilean crab bait scandal is easily addressed. Fishing companies simply need to provide fish bait for their fishermen. Other countries could boycott the import of Chilean crab. Like the tuna fishery in the Pacific, dolphins are dying to increase the profits of the fishing companies.

Three dolphin species in particular – Commerson's dolphin, the Chilean black dolphin and Peale's dolphin – are endangered by the Chilean king crab fishery. These species are found only in the Southern Hemisphere, have a very restricted range, and occur only in small numbers. Commerson's dolphin is found in Chilean waters and at the sub-Antarctic Kerguelen Island in the Indian Ocean; Peale's dolphin is restricted to coastal waters around the southern tip of South America and around the Falkland Islands; and the Chilean black dolphin is found only in Chilean waters. The original and present populations of all three species have never been assessed reliably, but because of their restricted distribution and the uncertainty of their numbers, the extent of their killing by crab fishermen is cause for grave concern.

The Chilean educational organisation Committee for the Defense of the Flora and Fauna of Chile (CODEFF) is heading efforts to stop the dolphin hunts. It believes that the government wants a short-term profitable fishery regardless of the consequences for the crab fishery or the dolphins. The dolphin hunts are a violation of Chilean law, several international conventions, and customary international law. But because of the economies of the crab fishery and the dim awareness of conservation within the Chilean government, the Committee believes that the hunting can be stopped only by pressure from governments that buy the crab.

## DOLPHINS TORTURED IN TAIWAN

In the Taiwan Strait, between Taiwan and mainland China, lies an archipelago of 64 small islands, the largest called Penghu. For over two centuries, local fisherman have driven dolphins ashore to be butchered and eaten. In a typical drive in March 1990, Penghu fishermen rounded up a mixed herd of 50 to 60 bottlenose dolphins and false killer whales (*Pseudorca*), and drove them through the narrow channel into Shakang Harbour. A few animals were sold to a Taiwanese Sea World, but several of the whales were cruelly slaughtered and killed. Beer bottles, stones, and steel rods were used to block blowholes and prise open wounds, and lances were driven into their eyes. One 300kg false killer whale, after hours of being teased and tortured, had its throat cut and bled to death on the dock. The remainder of the animals were confined by a net within a section of the dirty harbour, while the fishermen debated what to do with them.

Taiwanese residents who were members of the Hawaiian-based group Earthtrust contacted the Honolulu headquarters, and within a few days, an international team, led by Michael Bailey, arrived at Penghu to negotiate for the release of the remaining animals. They found that the mammals had been separated into three groups. The group remaining in Shakang Harbour were in a sad state, confined in a small space in a filthy harbour, with fishing boats leaking diesel and oil onto the surface of the water and continual dumping of rubbish, particularly plastics, from the shore. Another group of dolphins was kept in cleaner surroundings in a large concrete pool at the "Hawaiian Paradise" resort in Chikan Harbour. By the time the Earthtrust team arrived, two nursing calves had already died of starvation after being separated from their mothers. The third group of dolphins was in transit in Yeliu Harbour, prior to shipping to the oceanarium on mainland Taiwan.

Earthtrust removed the dead bodies and organised regular supplies of fish for the surviving dolphins in Shakang Harbour who were starving to death. The next challenge was how to secure their release.

During the week after their arrival, the team held meetings with the State Senator, the Mayor of Penghu County, teachers, businessmen, students, and Buddhist priests. They managed to convince the authorities that the dolphin kills were bad publicity, and that the release of some dolphins would be seen as partial atonement for the brutal killings which had already taken place.

The Mayor of the Hu Xi district offered almost US$20,000 to the fishermen for the purchase of 17 dolphins, hoping to use them as a tourist attraction. Earthtrust agreed to assist in caring for nine of the dolphins, if agreement could be reached to release three dolphins and the five remaining false killer whales. Although the fishermen were not happy about releasing the dolphins, the Mayor insisted, and to the cheers of bystanders, and the chanting of blessings by Buddhist monks, State Senator Chen Goei Miao untied the net and six fishing vessels escorted the cetaceans back to the open sea.

Michael Bailey believes that this could be the beginning of the end of Asian drive fisheries, and that by working with people, with an understanding of their culture and needs, cooperation can result. The Earthtrust presence at Penghu has focussed national attention on the dolphin drives, and senior officials in the Taiwanese Fisheries Department have since introduced legislation to provide greater protection for marine mammals. Fishermen must now obtain permits before they can take or injure any marine mammal.

# 7: DOLPHIN SLAUGHTER IN THE TUNA INDUSTRY

When US marine biologist and environmentalist Sam LaBudde worked undercover as a cook aboard a Panamanian tuna boat in 1988, he witnessed the full horror of the dolphin slaughter that frequently accompanies modern tuna fishing operations in the eastern Pacific Ocean. LaBudde documented for the first time, on video and in his diaries, the suffering and death of thousands of dolphins in a tuna fishing practice known as "fishing on porpoise", which has over the last 30 years killed between 6 and 12 million dolphins in the eastern Pacific. This senseless slaughter takes place merely to try to catch a few extra tuna, and in fact the tuna caught through this method amounts to only about 5 per cent of the world's total catch. Tuna can be successfully caught without killing any dolphins.

Fishing on porpoise is unique to the Eastern Tropical Pacific (ETP), a stretch of ocean extending from southern California to Chile and including about 11 million square kilometres (6 million square miles) of sea. In this area, schools of large yellowfin tuna often swim underneath groups of oceanic dolphins. The reason they swim together is not fully understood, but the tuna are believed to stay close to the dolphins to take advantage of their superior food-finding talents. Fishermen have long known of the association, and have traditionally used the presence of dolphins as a cue to finding schools of tuna. In the days when tuna were caught by the pole and line method, the dolphins were rarely involved or injured, but when the US introduced the purse seine fishing technique in the late 1950s, the slaughter of dolphins began on an unprecedented scale.

In purse-seine fishing, dolphin schools are often spotted from the air by the vessel's helicopter. They are then chased by both the helicopter and small high-speed boats which are also carried on board the seiner. The assumption is always made that a school of tuna is swimming underneath the dolphins. Tuna bombs, equivalent to small stun grenades, are frequently thrown from the air or boats, to further disorientate and scare the dolphins. When the dolphin school eventually stops, too confused or exhausted to swim any further, the

*Areas where dolphins are killed by purse-seine fishing for tuna.*

**Modern purse-seine boats, the so-called superseiners, fishing for tuna have huge nylon nets over 1.5 km (1 mile) long and 100 metres (325 feet) deep, manipulated by giant power machinery. They are highly sophisticated, crammed with electronics, and often carry their own helicopter. These custom-built vessels have been designed to catch only tuna – in huge quantities. The biggest are more than 1000 gross tonnes and can carry more than 1200 tonnes of tuna. Unlike the traditional methods of catching tuna by line or by lure, superseiners are able to scoop up entire schools, without a single fish escaping.**

*An American super-seiner with the huge net stacked on its stern, dory alongside and speedboats on the foredeck.*

> "Crew members are tearing dolphins out of the net and dumping them on the deck with little or no attention to whether they are alive or dead. Many of them just lie there helplessly until somebody manhandles them over the side of the boat. Finally the net is close-hauled and the skiff returns to the port side where the remaining floats in the water are draped over its side, forming a sort of bag between the two boats. It is packed with drowned dolphins. The crew members enter the water to push the dead bodies out of the net. Standing on the corpses they laugh and joke, holding the bodies of the babies over their heads like trophies, pitching them back and forth like footballs."
>
> *Sam LaBudde, US environmentalist,*
> *1 January, 1988*

The main dolphin species that swim in association with tuna are spotted, spinner and common dolphins. By 1979, US fisheries scientists were able to estimate some dolphin numbers in the ETP. Eastern spinner dolphins had been reduced to about 20 per cent of their original numbers, and the Costa Rican spinner dolphin (a subspecies) numbered only 9000. This supposedly protected sub-species continues to die in the tuna nets – Sam LaBudde witnessed 200 drown in a single net. Northern offshore spotted dolphins were around 40–50 per cent of their original numbers, and common dolphins about 60 per cent. Since 1979, the spotted dolphin has suffered the highest mortality, more females being killed than males. Of the females, 82.5 per cent have been found to be pregnant or lactating. The effects of the tuna fishery on other species in the ETP, such as the striped and bottlenose dolphin, have also been severe.

purse seiner steams up and sets its net around both dolphins and tuna, and then pulls the bottom closed, just like a drawstring purse. Many dolphins drown as the net is pulled and tightened towards the side of the seiner, and they become trapped in the closing mesh. Those that do escape, or are released by compassionate fishing captains and crew, are often caught again, and the same dolphins may often be chased to exhaustion and encircled with tuna nets many times each fishing season. Pregnant dolphins and mother/calf pairs are understandably the most severely affected by this ordeal.

The purse-seine tuna fleet in the Eastern Tropical Pacific is dominated by vessels registered in Mexico, the USA, Venezuela and Panama. In 1972 the US had by far the biggest fleet, with 98 of the largest class of tuna seiners, and was responsible for almost 90 per cent of the dolphin kill. Today US-registered vessels make up only one-third of the fleet, and account for less than 16 per cent of the total number of dolphin deaths. Mexico now has the largest purse-seine fleet, followed by the US and Venezuela.

Pressure by environmentalists in the US has meant that that country has for some years exerted some control over the industry by insisting that observers are placed on board US-registered boats. However, the powerful US tuna industry lobby has made sure that it has been given an annual "dolphin kill" quota. This bizarre concept makes a mockery of any claim that the dolphin slaughter by the tuna industry is incidental, but at least the quota provides a limited measure of control. The situation with non-US tuna vessels has been far worse, as most of them until very recently operated free of any regulations whatsoever. True records of the past dolphin kills by this sector of the industry can therefore only be estimated, and are likely to be very conservative.

Official figures do not usually include animals that escape or are released from the nets but have nevertheless been mortally wounded. Until very recently, observers were rarely on board to verify officially reported figures, and even if they were, attempts were often made to stop them witnessing the dolphin catch. Nor do the figures take into account the effect of the repeated chase and capture of dolphins during a fishing season.

Dolphin kills were suspected from the time the practice of fishing on dolphins began in 1959, but a secretive tuna industry for many years resisted all attempts to have observers placed on their boats, no doubt fearful of the outrage that would result if the truth were made public. Until 1971, dolphin mortality could be estimated only from analyses of vessels' logbooks – and the figures are probably underestimates. In the worst year, 1961, more than half a million dolphins were killed. This figure gradually declined to a low of about 25,000 in 1979 but has since climbed again, to around 125,000 in 1986.

Dolphins captured in nets can be freed if skippers and crew are sufficiently compassionate or are legally obliged to do so. One skipper who sought to reduce the carnage discovered that trapped dolphins could be released from nets by the use of a manoeuvre which came to be known as "backdown." The purse seine nets are made of large mesh in which it is easy for a dolphin to get its flipper or snout caught. However if a panel of fine mesh (called a Medina panel after the skipper who invented it) is incorporated into the back of the net, this can help save many dolphins. When the net has been pursed and brought to the side of the boat, the seiner can release the tension on the headrope of the net by the backdown procedure, which enables the back of the net with the finer mesh to sink and makes it easier for dolphins to escape, while the tuna continue to swim around in the net below. The US tuna industry was compelled by law to modify its nets and use the backdown procedure, which has significantly decreased the number of dolphins killed.

In many tuna sets most encircled dolphins are successfully released, but sometimes adverse weather conditions or equipment malfunctions can hamper the efforts of even the best-intentioned and most experienced crews. The resulting "disaster sets", when attempts to rescue the dolphins fail, can kill huge numbers. In 1986, 16 disaster sets accounted for 43 per cent of observed dolphin mortality by the US fleet and a single set that season killed 736 dolphins. In a "sundown set" dolphins are encircled late in the day, so that all or part of the backdown procedure is carried out during darkness. These dusk sets make it much harder for observers to see what is happening, and also make a successful backdown less likely. The kill rate is four times as high in the dark as during daylight. Not all vessels bother to try to release the trapped dolphins from the tuna nets, especially if there is no observer on board. Non-US vessels frequently make no attempt to save dolphins through the use of backdown.

Such slaughter of millions of dolphins is euphemistically classified as an example of "incidental catch". This misleading term tends to conceal the fact that dolphins are intentionally located, chased, harassed and encircled with a fishing net, from which attempts may not be made to release them.

Public outrage over the deaths of millions of dolphins in the 1960s prompted the introduction of a Marine Mammals Protection Act (MMPA) by the US in 1972, which was intended primarily to address the problem of dolphin kills in the tuna fishery.

Although the intention was that the allowable dolphin kill be gradually reduced each year to zero, since the introduction of the Act 800,000 dolphins have been killed by US purse seiners alone. Despite the vehement opposition to the passage of the Act by the tuna industry, steady progress was being made for a while by the US tuna fleet to reduce dolphin kills, until the election of ex-Californian governor Ronald Reagan as US President. Reagan was quick to succumb to pressure from the San Diego based tuna industry, and the MMPA regulations were relaxed. In 1981, an amendment by the US Congress permitted an annual US kill of 20,500 dolphins in tuna nets, completely overturning the original intention of the Act.

Once the new dolphin kill quota is reached, US seiners must stop carrying out sets on dolphins until the end of the year. However, there are always loopholes. For example injured and dying animals are not included in the limit the US tuna boats are officially allowed to kill each year. And observers on US-registered tuna boats claim that they are often pressured to falsify information about how many dolphins are "accidentally" killed during fishing operations.

The prime reason for encircling dolphins to catch yellowfin tuna is that the tuna which associate with dolphins tend to be larger, and command a higher market price. US fishermen in search of higher profit margins have increased the percentage of sets on dolphins every year since 1981. At this time the annual kill per US boat was less than 200, but by 1986, 94 per cent of all US sets were being "made on dolphins" and the kill figure had increased to more than 600. Meanwhile, many of the largest US purse-seiners had been re-flagged or sold to foreign investors. Thus fewer US vessels were responsible for killing an increasing number of dolphins between 1983 and 1986, while boats sold abroad were not affected by the imposition of dolphin kill quotas. The Marine Mammals Protection Act does at least go some way in limiting the dolphin kills, but since its introduction the tuna fishing fleet has become dominated by non-US vessels.

Non-US vessels are not bound by the MMPA, they are not required to carry any dolphin-saving equipment, and they rarely carry observers. Before 1986, Mexico, now the country with the largest purse-seine fleet, had not allowed any observers aboard its vessels. When, it finally did,

The US Marine Mammals Protection Act of 1972 stated that: ".... it shall be the immediate goal that the incidental kill or serious injury of marine mammals permitted in the course of commercial fishing operations be reduced to insignificant levels approaching zero mortality."

Although the incidental catch of dolphins in the purse-seine yellowfin tuna fishery in the ETP has indeed been greatly reduced since the 1960s, so also have the numbers of dolphins. Assessments of the permissible level of incidental catch should be based on the desirability of returning dolphin stocks to original levels, not holding them at a depleted level through a continuation of a high level of incidental kill.

reports showed that the Mexican tuna fleet had killed roughly 100,000 dolphins during that year – a rate four times greater than for US boats. The 1986 data destroyed the myth that the foreign kill rate was comparable to the US rate, and confirmed that the widely accepted official figure of 6 million dolphins killed by purse seiners over the past 30 years was a gross underestimate. The true number probably lies somewhere between 8 and 12 million animals.

The Inter-American Tropical Tuna Commission (IATTC) is the international agency responsible for carrying out research into the biology of tuna and recommending conservation measures to maintain fish stocks at "levels which will afford the maximum sustained catches." Nine countries originally entered the convention under which the IATTC functions, although only five (US, Panama, France, Japan, and Mexico) remained in 1986. Of the 16 countries presently fishing for tuna in the Eastern Pacific, only Panama and the US are currently members of the IATTC.

From 1967 to 1979, tuna catch quotas set by the Commission were approved by the IATTC countries. Since 1980, however, the member countries have failed to agree on the quotas recommended by the IATTC. In the absence of biologically sustainable quotas, yellowfin has been overfished. Stocks are now believed to be below the level which would allow the predicted maximum yield of 175,000 tonnes per year. In a declining fishery, extra pressure is thus placed on fishermen to catch the larger and higher value yellowfin which associate with dolphins.

Although the IATTC provides observers on purse-seiners, the programme was originally voluntary, and the tuna industry agreed to it only on the condition that observers are not allowed to report any violations. Furthermore, IATTC data are made available only to the US NMFS in an edited, summary form. The IATTC observer programme is thus a fairly pointless exercise, since the true data are not obtainable and violations are hushed up, proving the power of the tuna industry to silence the truth.

Until recently, no regulations relating to night sets applied to the non-US fleet. An NMFS regulation brought into force in January 1981 to disallow night sets by US boats was dropped after only 8 days because of pressure from the tuna industry. No further controls on the use of night sets were introduced until mid 1986, when US vessels were required to use effective lighting for dusk sets. This resulted in some success in lowering dolphin mortality, but it is still at least twice as high as during daylight hours.

Before 1982, less than half the tuna sets carried out by the US fleet were made on dolphins. When 4 years later the US fleet was ordered to stop making sets on dolphins once they had exceeded the annual kill quota, catch rates of tuna were not in fact noticeably affected. Yellowfin became elusive after the *El Nino* current change affected the availability of food supplies over the last two decades. This forced the purse-seine fleet to fish outside the eastern Pacific and they successfully caught tuna without encircling dolphins.

Some of the same US-registered super seiners operating in the southwest Pacific to catch skipjack tuna were the cause of considerable friction between the US Government and the Solomon Islands and Vanuatu in the South Pacific. These nations were incensed at the arrogant attitudes of unlicensed purse-seiners which plundered the tuna stocks within their 200-mile zones.

Corporate concern in the US tuna industry has been far more interested in maintaining profits than in saving dolphins, and they have gone to great lengths to protect their commercial interests. In 1980 alone, the American Tunaboat Association (ATA) spent over one million dollars to attack US fisheries scientists' assessments of dolphin mortality. They have brought numerous legal challenges to thwart the original intentions of the MMPA.

**"The fishermen resented the presence of a government observer and engaged in every possible form of harassment and coercion to ensure that I did not report the actual number of dolphins killed."**
*Affidavit filed June 1988 by Kenneth Marten, US fishing observer and research biologist*

Recognising that the increasing number of foreign vessels in the ETP was shifting the problem of dolphin incidental mortality away from their control, the US Congress in 1984 amended the MMPA. It now required that foreign nations exporting yellowfin tuna to the US adopt dolphin-saving programmes equivalent to the US' programme, and achieve a dolphin incidental mortality rate equivalent to that of the US fleet. Failure to show that these requirements had been met would result in a ban on the import of tuna from the nation involved. It took a full 4 years for the NMFS to draft the necessary regulations.

The NMFS, the US government agency charged with administering the MMPA, has often been accused by environmentalists of being in the pocket of the tuna industry. In 1984, during re-authorisation hearings on the Act, the US Congress directed the NMFS to develop regulations that would require an automatic embargo of tuna from any country which did not comply with the US dolphin-kill quota and requirements for dolphin rescue. It was a full 4 years before the regulations were released.

During this time, however, public outrage over the continued slaughter of tens of thousands of dolphins grew, spearheaded by LaBudde and the San Francisco-based Earth Island Institute. When the MMPA came up for amendment in 1988, environmentalists succeeded in forcing significant changes to the law. Besides requiring 100 per cent observer coverage for the US vessels, restrictions were also placed on sundown sets, and on encircling pure schools of certain severely depleted species of dolphins. Additionally, the use of explosives to herd dolphins was prohibited, and performance standards were introduced for skippers.

Dissatisfied with NMFS' slow progress in bringing the performance of foreign vessels into line with that of the US fleet, Congress further amended the MMPA in 1988 to specify that for a foreign fleet to avoid an embargo on its sales to the US market, the following progress would have to be made:

- By 1990, prohibition of setting on pure schools of certain species and conducting sundown sets;
- Independent observer coverage equal to that for US vessels (or at least sufficient for reliable estimation of dolphin mortality rates);
- An average incidental take rate no greater than twice that of the US fleet by the end of 1989 and no more than 1.25 times that of the US fleet by the end of 1990 and subsequent seasons.

On 17 January 1989, US District Court Judge Thelton Henderson, ruling on a lawsuit brought against NMFS by Earth Island Institute, issued an injunction against NMFS ordering the entire US tuna fleet to carry observers, and ordering all US tuna boats operating in the ETP without observers to "immediately return to port or otherwise immediately act to carry on board an official certified observer."

Judge Henderson's ruling had a profound impact. Foreign nations wishing to export tuna to the huge US market were compelled to rapidly develop observer programmes, dolphin-protection measures, education and training programmes for their fishing crews, and to achieve great improvements in their performance standards to make them comparable with the US fleet.

The September 1990 meeting of the Inter-American Tropical Tuna Commission marked a turning point. Members of all the nations purse-seining for tuna in the ETP, many of whom were no longer members of the IATTC, attended and adopted a dolphin conservation programme designed to bring the entire fleet into line with the US performance measures within 3 years. By 1992, only Mexico had failed to reach a level close to 100 per cent IATTC observer coverage for its tuna fleet.

Earth Island Institute continued its run of successful legal challenges against NMFS. A District Court ruled in January 1992 that the provisions of the MMPA required that any country which imported yellowfin tuna

**Yellowfin tuna in fact comprises only a small part of the huge US tuna market. In 1985, consumption of tuna in the US was 1.5 kg (3.3 lb) per person, of which white meat tuna (yellowfin) made up 0.3 kg (0.7 lb).**

**No longer able to conceal its victims, the US tuna fleet has been obliged to reduce the incidence of dolphin mortality through improved fishing methods. Dolphin deaths by US vessels fell from over 12,000 in 1989 to 5000 in 1990; despite an increase in numbers of sets by one-third, deaths were further reduced from 1000 in 1991 to 439 in 1992. 85 per cent of the sets resulted in no dolphin mortalities.**

**The most tragic and outrageous aspect of the tuna/dolphin story in the ETP is that the practice of encircling dolphins to catch tuna is entirely unnecessary. Yellowfin tuna taken inside the ETP make up about 8 per cent of the world's tuna catch. Even within the zone, good catches of yellowfin can be made without encircling dolphins.**

In the US, domestic pressures kept turning up the heat on the ETP tuna fleet. Representative Barbara Boxer, a Democrat from San Francisco, steered the Dolphin Protection Consumer Information Act through Congress in 1990. The Act set out criteria for labelling tuna and tuna products as "dolphin-safe" (i.e., caught without encircling dolphins), and provided for a fine of up to $100,000 for deliberate mislabelling.

Progress to protect dolphins continued to be made, however, through the United States Congress. The International Dolphin Conservation Act, enacted in October 1992 as a new Title III of the MMPA, provides a framework for further reductions in dolphin deaths in the ETP. The Act calls on the Secretary of State to enter into international agreements to establish a global moratorium on harvesting tuna by setting purse seine nets on dolphins, to take effect on 1 March 1994. Any country that fails to abide by the moratorium, or fails to meet its commitments, will be subject to an embargo of yellowfin tuna and other fish and fish products. Furthermore, after 1 June 1994, it will be unlawful to sell or transport any tuna or tuna product which is not "dolphin-safe".

In the US, a coalition of animal welfare groups is urging US consumers to stop buying tuna caught on dolphin. One approach developed by the environmental group Earthtrust has been the introduction of the voluntary "Flipper Seal of Approval", a sticker attached to cans of tuna signifying that the contents of the can have been caught without harming dolphins. About 830,000 tonnes of tuna is sold annually in the US, and canners have often failed to disclose on their labels where the tuna was caught, let alone under what conditions.

from a country which was subject to a primary embargo by the US, (for failing to reduce dolphin mortality, for example), would itself be the mandatory target of a secondary embargo by the US. The Court ruled that the Federal Government was not in compliance with the MMPA, and that a statutory embargo on imports of Mexican tuna should be imposed forthwith.

The foreign nations fishing for tuna in the ETP, however, have turned to the international community for support over the proposed imposition by the US of tuna import restrictions under the MMPA. In 1991, Mexico took its dispute over the tuna-dolphin issue to the world trade body, the General Agreement on Tariffs and Trade (GATT). A GATT disputes panel was established to hear Mexico's complaint that the embargo provisions of the MMPA, including the secondary embargoes on other importers of Mexican tuna, were inconsistent with the General Agreement.

In September 1991, in a bombshell decision, the GATT panel announced that the US embargo of Mexican tuna was not consistent with the General Agreement. Of particular concern to environmentalists was the finding that trade measures introduced by a country to protect animal life had no legitimacy in areas beyond their jurisdiction, and that the US could not meet their obligations under GATT while imposing secondary embargoes on countries handling Mexican tuna. Under GATT procedures, fortunately, dispute panel decisions must be adopted unanimously, and the US Senate immediately asked the President to block adoption of the panel's ruling. At present, the GATT challenge is in limbo, pending further negotiations between the US and Mexico, but a new challenge to the secondary embargo provisions of the MMPA is to be made by the European Community in 1993.

Foreign nations fishing in the ETP are heeding the message. In April 1992, a special meeting of the IATTC, involving all nations, agreed on a series of measures to progressively eliminate dolphin mortality. Limits on the maximum allowable annual number of dolphin deaths have been set, declining from 19,500 in 1993 to less than 5000 in 1999. Each vessel will receive a quota, derived by dividing the allowable number of dolphin deaths by the number of vessels fishing. The 1993 quota will be 183 dolphins per vessel.

Parallel with the political and legal campaign, Earth Island Institute developed a consumer awareness campaign that has also paid off spectacularly. In 1989, Starkist Seafood, the world's largest tuna canner with 35 per cent of the US market, was swallowed up by the multinational food giant H.J.Heinz. Earth Island Institute targeted Heinz with a publicity campaign, threatening a consumer boycott of their entire range of food products unless they ceased buying tuna caught by encircling dolphins. According to Anthony O'Reilly, Chairman of Heinz, the internal corporate debate was "epic, almost theological in tone". In April 1990, Starkist announced a new policy, under which they would no longer buy tuna which was not "dolphin-safe". The ban would not only apply to tuna taken by purse-seiners, but also to all tuna caught anywhere by gill nets, whether drift nets or set nets. Starkist forecast that prices of tuna would rise by a few cents per can, but expected that increased prices would be compensated for by improved sales, as environmentally-concious consumers opted for dolphin-safe tuna.

Within hours of Starkist's announcement, their major US competitors, Bumblebee and Van Camp, announced the introduction of similar policies. Although there have been difficulties in ensuring compliance with these policies, especially in the major canneries in Thailand and Indonesia, (where much of the world's tuna is now processed), there can be no doubt that the combination of political, legal and consumer pressure has finally saved the day for most of the dolphins in the Eastern Tropical Pacific. One can, however, only ponder at the ethics of an industry which for 30 years slaughtered dolphins in their millions to save a few cents on a can of tuna.

*Pilot whale carcasses lined up on the wharf, Faroe Islands. In 1988, 1690 pilot whales and over 600 dolphins were killed in the grynd.*
Dave Currey/Environmental Investigation Agency

*Opposite above*: *Dumped whale carcasses, Faroe Islands. Killing whales and dolphins once provided a valuable source of food for the Faroese, but today it has become more of a sport, and large quantities of the whale and dolphin meat finishes up on rubbish dumps.* Allan Thornton/Environmental Investigation Agency

*Opposite below*: *Dolphin blood stains the sea at Tatsunoshima Island, Japan, where dolphin hunts in the past have accounted for thousands of deaths.* Susie Cate

*Above*: *"Wall of death" nets present the newest threat to dolphins. Up to 60,000 kilometres of near-invisible drift-net are set in the North Pacific each night during a 6-month season, killing tens of thousands of dolphins a year – such as this baby common dolphin.* Robert Young/Earthtrust

*Above*: A drowned Dall's porpoise aboard a Japanese salmon drift-net factory ship. This fast-swimming North Pacific species frequently falls victim to drift-nets. NMFS

*Below*: A common dolphin drowned in a drift-net in the Tasman Sea. Japan and Taiwan are the culprits responsible for this indiscriminate killing. Brian Coffey

*Bottlenose dolphin. The bottlenose dolphin's brain is as large and complex as the human brain. Dolphin brains had already developed to this level of complexity millions of years before the appearance of humans.* Kim Westerskov

**Above**: Risso's dolphins. Several thousand of these dolphins die in gill-nets around the coast of Sri Lanka each year. The introduction of cheap nylon nets has enabled coastal countries rapidly to expand their fishing industries, often without accompanying controls.  Bob Talbot

**Opposite**: "Dolphins don't want us to have any purpose in our relations with them....They want us to be ourselves and they themselves and to meet as friends....Only after some quiet time with a dolphin do we enjoy letting it be in charge of the encounter, and see what it may decide to do next with us." (Chi-uh Gawain)  Kim Westerskov

**Left**: Common dolphins. Dolphins use sonar to communicate with each other, and their language is complex and elaborate. A dolphin emits a steady stream of sounds, such as whistles, squeaks, groans and clicks, through the top of its head.
Bob Talbot

**Above**: *A bottlenose dolphin surfacing to snatch a quick breath. Ancient Mediterranean cultures believed dolphins represented the vital power of the sea, and killing a dolphin was punishable by death.* Steve Dawson

**Left**: *For many people, their first encounter with wild dolphins is looking down from the bow of a travelling boat. Such wonderful experiences will become increasingly rare if dolphins continue to be slaughtered in their thousands every year.* Bob Talbot

# 8: DRIFT-NETS – STRIPMINING THE OCEANS

Until the end of 1992, 40,000–60,000 km (about 30,000–45,000 miles) of drift-net was set each night in the North Pacific Ocean – enough to encircle the planet and cross the Pacific for a second time. These "walls of death" were up to 15 metres (50 feet) deep, and they caught everything that swam into them.

Oceanic drift-nets have literally wiped out life over huge tracts of the world's oceans. Dolphins, large and small whales, sea birds and turtles, as well as the fish and squid swimming in the upper surface of the ocean at night, died each year in their tens or hundreds of thousands, victims of these enormous and near invisible webs of death. Their widespread use could have brought about the collapse of entire stocks of oceanic fish and caused lasting damage to marine ecosystems covering vast areas. Since their widespread introduction in the 1960s, drift-nets have already laid waste enormous areas of open ocean, especially in the North Atlantic and North Pacific. Drift-netting has become recognised as the most indiscriminate method of fishing ever devised.

As most drift-netting operations are carried out in international waters where little or no international agreements have been in force until recently, it has been extremely difficult to control this destruction of life on the high seas, or even to get an accurate picture of its magnitude. Japan, Taiwan and South Korea are the three countries most responsible for drift-netting, operating mainly in the North Pacific. Other nations that have used drift-nets include the US, Italy, and Spain, while Denmark in the 1970s had a large drift-net fishery for salmon in the North Atlantic.

Drift-nets were first developed by the Japanese, and have been used since 1905. Early drift-nets were made from natural fibres such as cotton and hemp, and were not large. But the large-scale manufacture of plastics after World War II encouraged FAO to sponsor the development of cheap, large, plastic nets, which were originally intended to help provide additional sources of protein for developing countries. Instead they became the favourite fishing method of several highly industrialised fishing nations, and the use of oceanic drift-nets has grown rapidly.

The ready availability of cheap, plastic, monofilament (single stranded) net revolutionised the distant water fishing fleets of Taiwan, South Korea and Japan. Old longline and squid jigging vessels were re-equipped with inexpensive nets instead of being retired, and sent out to return a few more seasons' profits. Japanese drift-nets in the 1970s were about 15 km (10 miles) in length, but soon became four times that length. The nets, released at dusk, drifted with the ocean's currents and winds, fishing the rich top 15 metres (50 feet) of the sea, to be retrieved the next day. The lack of international controls in the North Pacific Ocean, and the proliferation of the salmon, tuna, billfish, and squid drift-net fleets over the past two decades, resulted in the development of a North Pacific fishery so huge that during the 6-month season, the 1000 or so vessels involved deployed 3–5 million km (1.9–3.4 million miles) of netting.

Japanese authorities turned a blind eye to the rapid expansion of their drift-net fleet. In 1973, the Japanese Ministry of Agriculture and Fisheries, recognising the possible adverse effect of drift-nets on fish

"Earlier this year, I addressed a meeting of the Western Pacific Fisheries Council in Western Samoa. I discussed the evil of driftnetting as but one of a number of kinds of ecological terrorism. Everything I have seen and heard in the ensuing months reinforces my belief that driftnetting is a manifestation of an attitude which, unchecked, will in due course murder the only planet on which we can make our home."
*Peter Tali Coleman,
Governor, American Samoa
Speech to South Pacific Driftnet
Conference New Zealand,
November 1989*

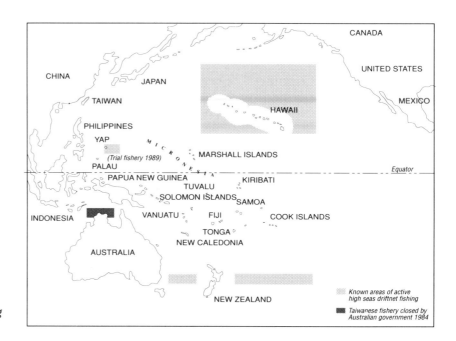

Known areas of active drift-net fishing in the Pacific Ocean.

**Dolphins and porpoises fall victim to drift-nets in large numbers because they cannot "see" them on their sonar. Although a dolphin's echolocation mechanism is remarkably sensitive, it probably cannot detect the thin strands of nylon which make up the mesh of oceanic drift-nets. The plastic floats at the top of the net could easily be detected by sonar, but in drift-nets, they are on the surface, where, even if detected, they would not give the dolphin any cause for alarm.**

**Some observer data on incidental catches on four vessels of the red squid fleet, over a total of 67 days' fishing through the 1980s, showed that 105 marine mammals died in 2870 km (2000 miles) of drift-net – one death for each 27 km of net. The 105 total included 12 common dolphin, 7 Dall's porpoise, 8 Pacific white-sided dolphin, and 56 northern right whale dolphin. If the annual quantity of net deployed within all North Pacific fisheries in a 6-month season is taken to be 3–5 million km (about 2–3 million miles), the total possible deaths of marine mammals would be about 109,000–181,500.**

stocks, issued an ordinance which limited the length of all Japanese drift-nets to 12 km (8.5 miles). At that time, their drift-netters were operating mostly within the Japanese 200-mile Exclusive Economic Zone (EEZ), and the development of larger vessels and the expansion of fishing grounds to include the high seas had not been expected. In theory, all Japanese drift-netters were restricted to 12-km nets, with a mesh size of 150 mm (6 inches), but in practice this regulation was completely ignored, and the high seas drift-net fleets operated with nets of up to 50 or 60 km (about 31 or 40 miles), and with a range of mesh sizes, as small as 80 mm (3.2 inches). The only concession made by these vessels to the ordinance was to break up their massive sets into several lengths of 10–12 km with a gap of 100–200 metres between each length of net.

Drift-net vessels, like the tuna boats fishing on dolphins, long stubbornly refused to take observers on board. For many years no reliable accounts existed of their effect on oceanic life. But according to a report by an observer from the US National Marine Fisheries Service, during a 6-week period in summer 1986, a single Japanese squid vessel working in Alaskan waters killed 53 dolphins and porpoises and 14 fur seals by entanglement in its nets. If this death rate were typical of the entire squid fleet, more than 125,000 marine mammals would have died annually in the drift-nets of the North Pacific squid fishery alone.

The fast-swimming Dall's porpoise has been particularly hard hit in the North Pacific and hundreds of thousands of animals over the last 20 years have been entangled in the giant drift-nets of the salmon, squid, and tuna fisheries. It is also deliberately hunted for human consumption in Japan. Estimates of annual deaths ranged up to 40,000 animals a year on the high seas of the North Pacific. The US Government in 1981 imposed a quota on Japanese drift-netters operating in Alaskan waters of 5500 porpoises a year.

Over 20 years ago, Japanese scientists were reporting that over 10,000 porpoises were being killed in the North Pacific each year in the drift-nets of the Japanese salmon fishery, and since then the drift-net fleet grew considerably. The Japanese drift-net fishery for squid alone accounted for between 7000 and 14,000 Dall's porpoise each year, and there were no reliable estimates for the incidental catch by

Taiwanese and Korean drift-netters in the squid, salmon, and tuna/billfish fisheries.

Japanese scientists, however, have been denying that drift-nets have had any significant effect on Dall's porpoise. In 1975, Dr Seiji Ohsumi, senior biologist at the Far Seas Research Laboratory, wrote that "many porpoises were incidentally caught by the salmon gill-net fisheries annually," but he saw "no evidence to show a decline in their population density." He concluded that the population size of Dall's porpoise was remarkably large (it was estimated as low as 790,000 in 1983), and that "the effect of incidental catch was negligible."

In this typical example of scientific doublespeak, the burden of proof is, as usual, thrown on to conservationists to show that a fishing technique has an unacceptable effect, rather than on the fishing nations to show that the method is ecologically sound. The coastal population of Dall's porpoise around northern Japan has also been drastically reduced by the huge growth in commercial harpooning, and this once-abundant species is clearly suffering a steep decline.

In 1988, the Hawaiian environmental group Earthtrust took a 13-metre (42-foot) sailboat into the North Pacific Ocean to document effects of the drift-net fishery for flying squid. Expedition biologist Sam LaBudde confirmed environmentalists' worst fears: "The toll was evidenced in the range of creatures we saw drowned in the nets. Dolphin, albatross, a leatherback sea turtle, numerous sharks, entire schools of tuna, sunfish, marlin, swordfish, salmon and flying squid. It is called a squid fishery, but the truth is that anything that moves near these nets is likely to be caught and killed." LaBudde noted that the quantity of non-target species taken during their time aboard was greater than the quantity of squid harvested.

LaBudde filmed entire schools of tuna trapped in the nets: "... the collective mass of their bodies temporarily pulling entire sections of net far below the surface. Here, in the seemingly endless expanse of clear blue, hundreds of fish hung strangely suspended in the water, the nets that held them all but invisible."

LaBudde also reported that the two drift-net vessel skippers to whom he had spoken in the North Pacific both admitted to periodically cutting loose large sections of net in which whales had become entangled. Whales enmeshed in a drift-net are condemned to a slow death from starvation or suffocation. LaBudde believes that drift-nets are the prime suspects for the disappearance of dozens of young humpback whales in the North Pacific, who have been failing to return to their Hawaiian breeding grounds in recent years. Their migration route to the Alaskan feeding grounds takes them through an area of ocean which is cluttered with drift-nets.

Drift-netting is another example of our inability as humans to establish a sustainable relationship with the planet. In the endless quest for short-term profits, fishing companies have used drift-nets in the full knowledge that dolphins, seals, turtles, and sea birds would be killed, often much faster than the target fish species. The environmental consequences of this stripmining of the oceans extend far beyond the inevitable depletion of the commercial resource. The collapse of marine mammal and sea-bird populations may have far-reaching consequences as the complex pattern of interrelationships among creatures in the marine ecosystem changes.

Some countries at least have recognised the extreme dangers of drift-net fishing. In 1986-87, the Canadian Department of Fisheries and Oceans carried out trials with squid drift-nets. During the trials with two vessels, 135 dolphins, porpoises, and small whales were killed, as well as over 700 sea birds. The Canadian Minister of Fisheries terminated the trials, and banned further drift-net fishing in Canadian waters.

"We encountered a baby common dolphin trapped only a few feet from the surface, its beak and tail flipper hopelessly wrapped in layer upon layer of nylon mesh. I couldn't help but imagine the scene of panic and desperation that must have taken place a few hours earlier – the young dolphin fighting and dying in a few frantic spasms, its grieving mother well able to defend her child from sharks but helpless against a silent, resisting wall of nylon."

*Sam LaBudde*

Robert Goldblatt, a US marine biologist, spent a month observing on a Japanese drift-net vessel fishing for skipjack tuna in the seas around Yap, in the Federated States of Micronesia. During that time, 24 sets killed 97 dolphins, 11 small whales, and 10 turtles. The whales that could be brought on board were filleted and the meat frozen, but the dolphins were thrown away. The catch of skipjack from the month's fishing was a mere 909 fish, weighing on average about 4 kg (9 lb) each. The quantity of whales and dolphins caught far outweighed the tuna.

The albacore tuna fishery in the South Pacific was thought by fisheries scientists to be fully exploited by trolling vessels, mainly from the US and New Zealand, and by longliners from Japan, Taiwan, and Korea. The sustainable yield from the fishery by these methods, which have little effect on other fish species, and no significant effect on dolphins, turtles, or sea birds, has been calculated as 45,000 tonnes per year – 35,000 tonnes of adult fish taken by longlines, and 10,000 tonnes of juveniles, taken by trolling. The drift-net catch of juvenile albacore in 1988-89 was estimated at between 29,000 and 49,000 tonnes, which is thought to be unsustainable.

Australia was also forced to take a stand on drift-netting when the establishment of the Australian Fishing Zone in 1979 brought under Australian jurisdiction a Taiwanese drift fleet that had been operating, since the mid 1970s, in what had previously been international waters in the Timor and Arafura Seas off northern Australia. By 1983, it was clear to the Australian authorities that the drift-nets were killing thousands of cetaceans each year. Australian scientists in 1983 estimated that 4700 dolphins had drowned in the giant nets in 22 months. Experiments with modified nets had no significant effect on the rates of entanglement. Between 1981 and 1985, roughly 10,000 dolphins drowned, mainly bottlenose, spinner, and spotted dolphins.

The Australian Government came under strong public pressure to take decisive action to protect the dolphin population from further depletion, and did so in 1986. By restricting the maximum length of pelagic gill-nets in the Australian EEZ to 2.5 km (1.6 miles), they effectively excluded the huge Taiwanese nets.

Attempts to introduce drift-nets into neighbouring New Zealand waters were more short lived. In 1981 four Taiwanese drift-netters undertook exploratory fishing for squid in Golden Bay at the northern end of New Zealand's South Island. The trials came to an abrupt end when local fisheries officers found the frozen remains of common dolphins and pilot whales on board the fishing boats. Under New Zealand's Marine Mammals Protection Act, the possession of marine mammals without a permit is a serious offence, and the drift-net trials were promptly terminated.

Little more was heard of drift-netting in the South Pacific until 1988, when for the first time, Taiwanese and Japanese vessels moved into the South Pacific and Tasman Sea in large numbers. Although a dozen or more Japanese drift-netters had been operating in the Tasman Sea for the previous 5 years, their presence had practically gone unnoticed. Then in November, 1988, the Japanese drift-net vessel *Sankichi Maru no. 18* caught fire in mid-Tasman, with the loss of all the crew. When New Zealand Search and Rescue authorities carried out several extensive air searches for survivors, it became apparent that as many as 50 or more Japanese drift-netters were concentrated in a small area of the Tasman Sea, fishing for albacore tuna.

The search for survivors from the *Sankichi Maru* was still in progress when the Taiwanese vessel *Delima 120* also got into difficulties about 1000 km (700 miles) east of Auckland. Her crew were all rescued, but it was discovered that the *Delima* was not, in fact, a water-carrier, as had originally been claimed, but a support ship for a massive fleet of between 60 and 130 Taiwanese drift-net vessels, fishing for albacore tuna along an area of oceanic upwelling known as the Subtropical Convergence Zone, stretching across the South Pacific in a narrow 300-km (200-mile) band from south of the Cook Islands to south of French Polynesia. Horrified fisheries officials in the South Pacific suddenly realized the extent of the drift-net fleet newly arrived in their region. Up to 180 boats were setting as much as 8000 km (5000 miles) of net each night during the 4-month season.

Although no reports on incidental killings of small cetaceans in the new Tasman/South Pacific drift-net fishery were provided by the Taiwanese, Japanese, or Korean governments, there could be little doubt of the damage being done.

In New Zealand, an unlikely coalition of government scientists, harbour boards, fishermen, and environmental groups pressured the government to take firm action to resist the invasion of the drift-netters. Japanese drift-net vessels, frequent visitors to New Zealand ports during the previous year, now found themselves subjected to lengthy searches by fisheries officers hunting for dolphin and whale remains. Efforts to control the drift-net fleets were boosted by the news that on 8

April 1989 the state legislature of Hawaii, in a bold move, had introduced legislation to ban the use and possession of drift-nets within the state's EEZ. New Zealand rapidly followed suit.

On 26 May 1989, the then Deputy Prime Minister, Mr Geoffrey Palmer, announced that not only would the use of drift-nets be banned inside the New Zealand EEZ, but also their possession. Drift-netters wishing to move from fishing grounds in the Tasman to those in the South Pacific would not be allowed to pass through New Zealand waters without risking confiscation of their vessels and a substantial fine. In a strongly worded statement signed by six Cabinet Ministers, Palmer described drift-net fishing as "abhorrent", and offered the use of New Zealand aircraft and naval vessels to assist neighbouring Pacific states who might wish to take similar action.

The New Zealand stand was swiftly followed by Australia, which also banned the possession and use of drift-nets in their 200-mile EEZ. In June 1989, delegations from Japan, Taiwan, and South Korea attended a meeting of the South Pacific Forum Fisheries Agency (FFA), to discuss the effects of the rapid expansion of the use of drift-nets in the region. Of particular concern to most of the members of the FFA was the effect of the drift-netters on the albacore tuna resource, which plays a major role in many Pacific economies.

Despite predictions from the FFA that drift-netting would bring about the collapse of albacore stocks within a few years, the Japanese delegation steadfastly refused to make any concessions. Drift-netting, they declared, was here to stay, and there were no scientific grounds to believe that there was any significant incidental catch of marine mammals, turtles, or sea birds in the South Pacific. Since the Japanese and Taiwanese refused to supply any data on the albacore drift-net fishery, it was hardly surprising that no information on incidental dolphin catches had come to light. Towards the end of the 3-day FFA meeting, the Japanese, "in a spirit of goodwill and co-operation", offered to hold the drift-net fleet for 1989-90 to the same level as the previous season – 60 vessels. This represented a four-fold increase on the previous maximum fleet size before 1988-89.

Japanese intransigence, however, served only to harden the resolve of the island nations of the South Pacific. At the July 1989 gathering of Heads of State on the island of Tarawa, in Kiribati, the South Pacific Forum placed the use of drift-nets in the South Pacific as its most important agenda item – the first time that an environmental issue had topped the agenda at a political gathering in the South Pacific.

The Tarawa Declaration, published at the conclusion of the Forum meeting, condemned drift-net fishing as "indiscriminate, irresponsible and destructive", and "not consistent with international legal requirements in relation to rights and obligations of high seas fisheries conservation and management and environmental principles". The Declaration further resolved to call together an urgent meeting of regional diplomatic, legal and fisheries experts to develop a Convention to establish a South Pacific zone free of drift-net fishing, and called upon Japan and Taiwan "to abandon immediately their damaging drift-net operations."

The South Pacific nations agreed to meet in Wellington, New Zealand, in November 1989, to conclude a convention to ban the use of drift-nets in the entire region. Geoffrey Palmer, Prime Minister of New Zealand, promptly announced his intention to call for a global ban on drift-netting during his address to the United Nations General Assembly in New York in October.

In a belated attempt at conciliation, the Japanese Government announced in mid September that the drift-net fleet in the Tasman Sea for the 1989-90 season would be reduced to 20 vessels, in the hope that the South Pacific nations could be diverted from their diplomatic assault. Palmer responded that the cut in vessel numbers was a positive move, but fell far short of the ban which remained the objective of the Pacific Island nations.

Nevertheless, the Japanese fleet arrived in the Tasman as promised, to be met by the new Greenpeace flagship, *Rainbow Warrior II*. The Greenpeace ship soon located the Japanese drift-net fleet, monitoring and documenting on film the catches in the drift-nets. Dolphins were frequently observed in the nets, and Greenpeace estimated that even the reduced fleet of 20 vessels probably killed some 4600 dolphins during the season.

The prompt action by South Pacific countries to deal with the drift-net plague provided a marked contrast to the situation in the North Pacific high seas, where the US had been dragging its heels as the Asian drift-net fleets continued to pillage the salmon, tuna, and squid resources, and kill tens of thousands of marine mammals and hundreds of thousands of sea birds, many of them in Alaskan fisheries waters. A change in US policy was, however, signalled by the passage through the US Congress of the Drift-net Monitoring, Assessment And Control Act in 1987. The Act requires the Secretary of Commerce to report to Congress on numerous aspects of drift-net fishing in the North Pacific, especially as it relates to the marine resources of the US.

Because of their incidental catch of thousands of Dall's porpoise each year, Japanese drift-net vessels fishing for salmon off Alaska were subject to the provisions of the US MMPA. The MMPA generally prohibits the killing of marine mammals in US waters, but contains an important exception – the Secretary of Commerce can authorise the accidental drowning of marine mammals in commercial fishing operations. The Secretary cannot, however, allow the incidental take of any species in danger of significant depletion or extinction.

US scientists in the early 1980s, estimated an "acceptable level of kill" for the drift-net fishery of 5500 Dall's porpoise each year in Alaskan waters. Japanese salmon drift-netters fishing off Alaska were therefore allowed this figure as an annual quota as incidental catch. When the permit came up for renewal in 1986, Commerce Secretary Malcolm Baldridge issued a general permit for the drift-netting to continue. He had decided that stocks of Dall's porpoise would not be significantly depleted by such a move, but he was unable to make such a claim for northern fur seals and sea-lions.

Environmental groups successfully appealed against the issue of the general permit, and in July 1987, won an injunction which cut short the salmon season for the drift-net fleet. Japanese salmon fishing operations in 1988 were totally blocked by the injunction. Finally, after further lengthy legal battles, the Supreme Court issued a landmark decision in January 1989, and refused to allow the government to permit continued use of drift-nets off the Alaskan coast.

In 1989 the global nature of the drift-net plague was for the first time widely recognised. In May, South Africa, concerned at the proliferation of the Japanese drift-net fleet around the edges of its 200-mile EEZ, banned the use and possession of drift-nets in its EEZ.

In July, a simmering dispute in Europe became public, when the Greenpeace campaign vessel, *Sirius*, led a flotilla of 40 Spanish longline fishing boats into the port of Cartagena in south-east Spain. Environmentalists and fishermen were protesting at the devastating effects of the Spanish and Italian drift-net fishery for swordfish. Swordfish is a great delicacy in Europe, and has been traditionally caught on longlines, although catch rates have been declining in recent years.

The introduction of large-scale drift-nets into the Mediterranean has greatly boosted the catch of swordfish, according to fishermen. Many Mediterranean fishermen have been subsidised into the use of drift-nets through the European Community, which has been paying them to convert from bottom trawling – supposedly because of its detrimental effects on the seabed. In 1988, 30–40 Spanish vessels were operating out of Algeciras and Almeria, and according to some estimates, as many as 800 Italian and French drift-net vessels, with a total net length exceeding 15,000 km (about 10,000 miles), were fishing in the Mediterranean. The burgeoning European drift-net fleet is thought to have killed as many as 4000 dolphins in 1989, and at least 23 sperm whales during the previous three years.

The Milan-based Centre for Cetacean Studies, in association with several other wildlife and research groups, has petitioned the Italian Government for an end to the swordfish drift-net fishery, warning that the cetacean populations of the Italian seas would otherwise be at risk of extinction by the year 2000.

As the extent of drift-net fishing around southern Europe became more apparent, public outrage grew. In both Spain and Italy, emergency regulations were introduced to impose a temporary moratorium on drift-net use, pending governmental investigations.

In August 1989 Greenpeace drew attention to the swordfish fishery in US waters off the New England coast. Swordfish in the Georges Bank fishing grounds in the north west Atlantic Ocean have traditionally been taken by harpoon, but heavy fishing pressure has driven stocks to an all-time low, and some boats have turned to the use of drift-nets. Although the nets are much shorter than those employed in the North Pacific, and have a much larger mesh, they are devastatingly effective at catching dolphins. The mile-long nets hang in the water to a depth of 30 metres (100 feet), forming a much deeper net curtain than the squid and salmon nets of the open ocean.

In September 1989, the South Atlantic Fishery Management Council, one of eight US Regional Fishery Management Councils, voted to prohibit the use of drift-nets for swordfish in southern US Atlantic waters. The Council also urged the New England Fishery Management Council to introduce a similar ban, and called on the US delegation to the International Commission for the Conservation of Atlantic Tunas (ICCAT) to support a resolution to prohibit the use of drift-nets for all tuna and other species under the jurisdiction of ICCAT.

By October 1989, therefore, the time was right for a concerted diplomatic initiative against drift-net fishing. New Zealand Prime Minister Geoffrey Palmer's speech to the United Nations General Assembly that month called for a global ban, and spelt out the effect that drift-netters were having on the fragile fishing-based economies of the South Pacific. His address sparked an international campaign, aimed mainly at Japan (South Korea has only observer status at the UN, Taiwan is not represented at all). The first hurdle to be overcome was the development of a joint US/New Zealand resolution which would meet not only the concerns of the South Pacific nations which were at the forefront of the initiative, but also would not alienate the US, whose powerful political muscle would be required to gain the necessary support.

For some weeks, it seemed that the joint US/NZ resolution on drift-netting would founder in the mire of State Department compromise, as successive US proposals were rejected as too weak by the New Zealanders. Only after pressure from US Secretary of State James Baker, was a draft resolution agreed with New Zealand, which called for:

- An immediate ban on drift-netting in the South Pacific.
- The provision of accurate data by fishing nations.
- A moratorium on the use of high seas drift-nets from mid 1992 onwards, unless they could be shown to have a negligible effect on marine living resources (diplomatic language for marine mammals and sea birds).

The resolution, co-sponsored by Australia, New Zealand, and 14 other states, including several Pacific Island nations, was presented to the Second Committee of the United Nations General Assembly in November 1989. Japan, faced with a diplomatic assault on several fronts, responded with a resolution which shifted the onus of proof – drift-netting could be banned if scientific evidence clearly showed that the effects on fish stocks and cetaceans were "not sustainable".

An intensive bout of lobbying by both sides followed during the next month, both in New York and in capital cities all over the world. The opening salvo was fired by Japan, which produced a slick 20-minute video optimistically titled "The Truth About Drift-netting." The film flatly denied that there was any problem with dolphin entanglements in drift-nets, saying that the nets were always set in the direction of the prevailing currents, and as marine mammals generally swam with the currents, entanglement was unlikely.

The man behind the video and the Japanese public relations offensive in New York was Alan Macnow, long-time lobbyist for the Japan Whaling Association, and a familiar figure at IWC meetings. Even Macnow's legendary skills, however, were unable to persuade any countries to co-sponsor the Japanese resolution.

Nevertheless, the Macnow-inspired video did a sufficiently good job of muddying the waters to give the Japanese some hope of diverting the main thrust of the US/New Zealand resolution. After many long hours of negotiations between the key delegations, however, and increasing support among South American and African countries for a total ban on drift-nets, a compromise text was agreed which involved substantial concessions by Japan.

The text which was finally agreed on 11 December 1989 provided for:
- A freeze on further expansion of any drift-netting on the high seas outside the South Pacific.
- A moratorium on the use of large-scale drift-nets in the South Pacific from mid 1991, at least until the conclusion of a management regime for southern albacore tuna.
- A global moratorium on drift-net fishing on the high seas, including the North Pacific, from mid 1992, unless scientific evidence can be provided to demonstrate that drift-net use does not pose an unacceptable hazard to marine living resources.

The Japanese thus gained a couple of years to phase out their use of drift-nets, and retained the hope that their research scientists might be able to hide the truth about drift-net fishing. By providing Japan with the opportunity to save face and make an orderly withdrawal from drift-net fishing, the UN Second Committee bound them into a commitment to cease drift-net operations in the near future – an astonishing achievement for a campaign which had only really gathered momentum 10 months earlier, with the sinking of the *Sankichi Maru*.

As more information became available many more countries came to understand the damage caused by oceanic drift-nets. Because the nets were usually deployed many hundreds or even thousands of kilometres from shore, few but their crews had ever witnessed the damage inflicted on the marine ecosystem by the drift-net vessels. The true incidental catch of large and small whales, dolphins, and porpoises will never be known, but wherever drift-net fleets went they undoubtedly left thousands of dead cetaceans in their wake.

Over the next 12 months the major drift-net nations, as expected, mounted a stiff resistance to the impending ban, claiming that no scientific evidence existed to show that the incidental catch of marine mammals in driftnets was not sustainable. Their task was made all the harder, however, as the results became available from the observer programmes developed by the US as a consequence of the 1987 Driftnet Impact Monitoring, Assessment and Control Act.

In June 1991, a review of the North Pacific Ocean driftnet fishery was carried out in Sidney, British Columbia, attended by scientists from the US, Canada and the Asian driftnet nations. The meeting concluded that the number of northern right whale dolphins had declined significantly because of the take in driftnets, and that Pacific white-sided dolphins could experience similar declines if driftnet fishing continued unabated.

The Sidney meeting confirmed the worst fears of the nations sponsoring the United Nations initiative, and kept the diplomatic pressure firmly on the driftnetters. Resistance crumbled, and in December 1991, 30 nations, including Japan, cosponsored UN General Assembly Resolution 46/215, which called on the international community to:

- Reduce large-scale driftnet fishing effort by 50 per cent by 30 June 1992;
- Ensure that drifnet fishing on the high seas did not expand into new areas;
- Fully implement a global moratorium on all large-scale driftnet fishing on the high seas by 31 December 1992.

To strengthen efforts to support and implement the global moratorium on driftnetting, US President George Bush signed into law the High Seas Driftnet Fisheries Enforcement Act in November 1992. The Act not only denied port facilities to any vessel involved in driftnetting after the end of 1992, but more importantly prohibited the import of fish from countries engaged in driftnet fishing contrary to the moratorium.

By the end of 1992, Japan, Korea and Taiwan had all agreed to comply with the terms of the UN Resolution, and cease driftnetting in international waters. What is now required is a greater commitment by all fishing nations to sustainable alternatives for harvesting the oceans' bountiful resources — methods such as squid jigging and tuna trolling, which have a negligible effect on non-target species.

# 9: GILL-NETS – THE QUIET MASSACRE

```
THE GILL-NET

Modern plastics technology has made possible the mass production
of cheap and durable nylon nets, which were initially developed to
provide an affordable and effective fishing method to aid developing
countries.
    Gill-nets are almost always constructed of thin nylon monofilament
or multifilament line, knotted to form a meshed net. The net has
weights along the bottomline, and floats along its topline to hold it
vertical in the water. The size of the mesh varies depending on which
fish species the net is supposed to catch, as does the length and
depth of the net. The strands are so fine that they usually cannot be
detected by cetacean sonar, unlike the older type of multifilament
cotton nets. Fish encountering the modern nylon nets attempt to
swim through the near-invisible mesh and become entangled, usually
by the gills – hence the name gill-net.
    Depending on the target species, the net is set at the bottom and
anchored, or set at the surface and left to drift with the wind and
current. Oceanic drift-nets can be enormous, up to 56 km (35 miles)
long, and are causing considerable concern because of their effects
on marine mammals, sea birds, and fish stocks. Set gill-nets are much
shorter, and are used mostly in shallow coastal seas, where they are
anchored to the seabed.
    Gill-net entanglement affects coastal dolphin and porpoise species
worldwide, and these animals' low reproductive rates make them ill-
suited to cope with this type of threat.
```

Since humans first developed methods of catching fish, the occasional
dolphin or porpoise has probably fallen unwitting victim to net, hook,
or in more recent times, trawl net. But now these incidental catches
have come to present a major danger to cetacean populations. Dr
Stephen Leatherwood, of the UN Environment Programme, estimates
that between a half to one million small cetaceans each year are caught
in set-nets. Many countries do not compel fishermen to report the
accidental capture of small cetaceans in their nets, so significant
catches may go unnoticed for years.
    The problem is often the worst in developing countries such as Sri
Lanka, where the introduction of cheap nylon nets has often enabled
coastal states to rapidly expand their fishing industries. In 1985, a
report to the IWC Scientific Committee revealed that more than 40,000
dolphins were being killed each year as a result of incidental catches in
set-nets around Sri Lankan coasts. This huge dolphin kill spells a dire
warning of the effect of introducing modern plastic gill-nets into
developing coastal fisheries, without accompanying controls. There are
many fisheries throughout the Indian sub-continent and the Sri Lankan
operation is the only one in this area so far to have been carefully
studied. It is reasonable to assume that an alarming number of dolphin
deaths must be occurring around the coasts of the continent which are
as yet unreported.

Dr Bill Perrin, who compiled the authoritative International Union for the Conservation of Nature (IUCN) Action Plan for the conservation of dolphins and porpoises, identified the convening of an international workshop on gill-nets and cetaceans as one of the Plan's highest priorities. Participation by developing nations which are expanding the use of gill-nets in their coastal waters was a key feature of the workshop, which was held in La Jolla, California, under the auspices of the International Whaling Commission in October 1990.

Fishermen in many countries catch dolphins in set-nets, but are not required to report the deaths to fisheries authorities. Even in countries with laws that provide some degree of protection for marine mammals, fishermen are often reluctant to report incidental catches of dolphins or porpoises because they fear having restrictions placed on their use of set-nets.

In the Gulf of Maine, commercial mackerel fishermen have kept silent for years about the number of harbour porpoises dying in their nets. The truth was revealed only by chance, when a journalist for the US magazine *Sports Illustrated* happened to be aboard a boat when it hauled up seven dead porpoises, caught in a single set. The *Sports Illustrated* report confirmed scientists' suspicions that as many as 600 porpoises each year were dying in entanglements in the Gulf, out of a total population for the East Coast of the US and Canada of perhaps only 8000. The annual kill is thought to be far greater than could be replaced by the harbour porpoise's slow rate of reproduction.

Because it inhabits coastal waters in heavily populated and fished areas, the harbour porpoise has suffered greatly in recent years. They were once widely distributed throughout the North and Baltic Seas, but populations here have rapidly declined as a result of environmental contaminants such as pesticide residues and toxic industrial wastes. Until recently, they were killed in their thousands by Turkish hunters in the Black Sea and they are still being actively hunted in Greenland, where about 1000 porpoises are harpooned or shot each year. Now harbour porpoises face the additional threat of coastal gill-nets.

Tom Polacheck, of the US NMFS, who has been closely involved with the harbour porpoise entanglement problem, believes that the incidental taking of harbour porpoise is an example of the problems that face both the marine scientist and society, in that both marine animals and commercial fisheries are highly valued and represent issues of concern to various segments of society.

Canadian Professor David Gaskin's 20-year involvement with harbour porpoise has led him to examine the conflict between gill-net and small cetacean worldwide. He has also been a licensed gill-netter himself. He is convinced that the introduction of lightweight monofilament nylon into coastal gill-net fisheries has been a global disaster for many coastal species of dolphins and porpoise. In a recent letter to an amateur gill-netter in New Zealand, Gaskin said: "Animals like Hector's dolphin, with a very low reproductive rate, are disappearing steadily all over the world... The New Zealand controversy is not a unique situation. In almost all cases, the sustained incidental catch is caused by gill-nets, either set or drifters, or by lost ghost nets."

Although a number of reports had identified gill-nets as the prime culprit in causing the declining populations of coastal dolphins all over the world, it was not until the La Jolla workshop that the international scientific community focussed its attention on the problem. The conclusions of the workshop confirmed an authoritative report prepared for Greenpeace in 1985 by Simon Northridge of the Marine Resources Assessment Group of Imperial College, London, and Professor Georg Pilleri, a respected dolphin expert. The report identified a lengthy list of incidental catches of dolphins and porpoises in gill-nets, of which the following are only a selection. The numbers of cetaceans caught in

"There is hardly a civilised Fisheries Department in the world that would not ban this sloppy, terrible method of fishing if the politicians would show some backbone."

*Professor David Gaskin,
University of Guelph, Ontario*

gill-nets through incidental catch need not be large to severely affect some species, nor are catches confined to developing countries. Many of the species involved are listed internationally as endangered. The Convention of Trade in Endangered Species (CITES) has since 1973 aimed to protect species threatened by international trade, and lists endangered animals in three appendices according to the degree of threat they face. Appendix 1 is the most endangered list, and animals on it may not be traded for commercial purposes.

- In the Gulf of California, the use of gill-nets may have pushed the vaquita or Gulf of California porpoise to the edge of extinction. Never an abundant species, and very restricted in its distribution, it is probably the most endangered dolphin of all.

  In the early 1970s a gill-net fishery developed in the Gulf of California for the totoaba fish, and the nets also caught many vaquita (also known as cochito). After less than 5 years of this fishery operating in the Gulf, not only were the totoaba fish stocks in danger of collapse but the vaquita population was also severely depleted. In 1975, the Mexican government banned totoaba fishing, but the damage had already been done. An unknown number of vaquita, probably in the hundreds, had already been lost. An extensive survey of the Gulf in 1986 sighted only 31 animals. Because the porpoise is such a slow breeder, there may not be enough individuals left to guarantee the survival of the species.

  Despite the international publicity generated by the 1986 research effort, the plight of the vaquita is still not a major concern of the Mexican government. However a grant from the US Center for Marine Conservation enabled Mexico to monitor the Gulf of California fishery in 1988. A sample of the fishermen operating the 816 boats in the area found that 93 per cent used the type of gill-net which entangles vaquitas. Most of them fish legally for sharks, but some still illegally net totoaba, and the 125- and 150-mm (5- and 6-inch) mesh nets they use continue to drown the vaquita.

  The remaining numbers of vaquita cannot be estimated (even the external appearance of the animal was not fully described until 1985). Nevertheless, the total population is obviously very small, possibly less than 100, and unlikely to be more than 1000. In its action plan to save threatened cetaceans the Cetacean Specialist Group of IUCN has given the highest priority to a study which would monitor the scattered gill-net fisheries in the Gulf of California.

- The tucuxi is one of the hump-backed dolphins. It is found throughout the Amazon and Orinoco basins, and as far north as the Atlantic coast of Central America. There are at least two separate populations, one coastal and the other freshwater. No reliable population estimates exist. Because of its coastal habitat, incidental catches in gill-nets are widespread but the effects on the population are unknown. The tucuxi is currently listed in Appendix 1 of CITES.

- The Indo-Pacific hump-backed dolphin, also listed in CITES Appendix 1, is found throughout the Indian Ocean, and as far north as Canton in China and as far east as Sydney, Australia. In Asia, the dolphin is confined mainly to mangroves, where it feeds on shrimps, whereas it is more likely to be found around rocky shores in other parts of its range. It falls victim to gill-nets throughout its range, with the largest mortality thought to be in Pakistan and the Indus delta, although no reliable figures are available. Destruction of the dolphin's mangrove habitat in much of its Asian range may be a particularly grave threat. The exact numbers of animals caught in nets are unknown, but available statistics show incidental captures to be widespread throughout the region, and these mortalities may have a considerable effect on local populations.

- The Atlantic hump-backed dolphin is found along the West African coast, from Mauritania to Angola. It is rare, and the population size is unknown. Since the dolphin is caught in shark nets, other unreported deaths probably occur all along the coast. This species is also listed on CITES Appendix 1.

- Risso's dolphin is widely distributed throughout the world. The most serious incidental catch is in the coastal net fisheries around Sri Lanka, where an unknown number, probably in the thousands, are drowned each year.
- Spinner dolphins are frequently taken in set-nets around Sri Lanka, where about 17,000 are estimated to be incidentally caught each year.
- Common dolphins are incidentally taken in fisheries all over the world – at least 8000 animals each year die in gill-nets and seine-nets.
- Burmeister's porpoise has been caught incidentally in gill-net fisheries in Peru for many years. As long ago as 1975, 120 tonnes of porpoise meat was sold annually in Peru.
- The largest interbreeding population of Hector's dolphin around Banks Peninsula in New Zealand, lost 230 of its estimated 760 members through entanglement in set-nets between 1984 and 1988.
- A close relative of Hector's, the Chilean black dolphin, is caught in surface gill-nets all along the Chilean coast, its only habitat. Annual catches have been estimated at 1500, from a total population believed to number in the low thousands.
- Estimates of the number of small cetaceans taken deliberately and accidentally around the coastline of France are as high as 3000 animals each year.
- In addition to the several hundred harbour porpoises which die each year in the set-net fishery in Canada and the north-eastern US, as many as a thousand more are dying in set-nets in the North Sea and Greenland.
- Local populations of some dolphins have been severely affected by the use of shark nets to protect bathers. In both South Africa and Queensland, shark nets have killed hundreds of dolphins, with the worst affected being hump-backed, common, and bottlenose species.

Northridge and Pilleri list many more instances of dolphin entanglement in set-nets. All the data published on the effect of gill-nets on small cetaceans probably represents a conservative estimate of the number of deaths. Dolphins and porpoises are being entangled in monofilament death traps throughout the world, and a great many drownings go unreported.

A more concerted action by governments to address this quiet massacre might have been expected, but part of the problem is the lack of a single international forum to deal with the management of small cetaceans. In most countries the fishing industry has a powerful political lobby, with jobs and profits taking priority. International action is now needed to ban the use of gill-nets by amateur fishermen. Even in protein-starved, less-developed countries, the use of monofilament nets ultimately does more harm than good – their catching efficiency rapidly depletes many fish resources.

Ironically, the quest for profits may ultimately come to the dolphins' rescue. In the international seafood trade, freshness and appearance of the product is becoming increasingly important. Fish caught in gill-nets are generally regarded as being of poorer quality, because they are often dead for many hours before coming aboard the fishing vessel. Gill-nets are also generally much less selective than most other fishing methods, and often catch not just marine mammals but many other non-target fish species. There is thus a trend towards phasing out their use in commercial fisheries in favour of other methods like longlining and trolling, which land a better quality product, without the unwelcome incidental catch of non-target species.

# 10: LAST-MINUTE REPRIEVE FOR THE DOWNUNDER DOLPHIN

Hector's dolphin is one of the four species of the genus *Cephalorhynchus*, all of which are found in different areas of the Southern Hemisphere at temperate latitudes. The other species are Commerson's dolphin, Heaviside's dolphin, and the Chilean black dolphin. All are small, but Hector's is the tiniest, reaching only 1.4 metres (4 feet 6 inches) maximum length, and weighing no more than 40–47 kg (88–103 lb) when fully grown. Its size and distinctive black and white markings have earned it the title of panda of the dolphin world, which portrays its lovable, almost cuddly qualities.

Until recently, little was known about the tiny and endearing Hector's dolphin, found only in the coastal waters of New Zealand. Nobody suspected that a significant proportion of the small population was being caught and killed each year in fishing nets. Now Hector's is in the limelight not only in New Zealand but also internationally, as efforts to save this unique species are making it one of the conservation success stories of the world.

The discovery of the plight of Hector's dolphin in 1986 was a fateful coincidence. Virtually no information existed on the biology and distribution of the dolphin, until two Auckland University graduates decided to make the species the subject of their doctoral theses. Their choice may have made the difference between survival and extinction for Hector's dolphin. The story demonstrates the urgent need for similar studies to be undertaken in other parts of the world to determine the status of the many other dolphin species about which we know so little.

The two students, Stephen Dawson and Elisabeth Slooten, carried out a 6400-km (4000 mile) survey of the dolphin's known habitat, covering most of New Zealand's South Island and the lower half of the west coast of the North Island. They estimated the total population at 3000–4000 animals and discovered that almost a quarter lived around Banks Peninsula, near the South Island's largest city, Christchurch. The seas in this area have since the mid 1970s supported many commercial fishermen who set nets around the coast to supply the local fish and chip trade.

Dawson and Slooten discovered that these nylon monofilament gill-nets, up to 3000 metres (9750 feet) in length, were responsible for the deaths of far more dolphins than had ever been officially reported, and that the local dolphin population was in fact declining rapidly. Fishermen willingly co-operated with the students, passed on information about dolphin sightings, and even handed over the bodies of dolphins accidentally taken in their fishing nets. Many Hector's dolphins were also falling victim to the nets of recreational fishermen who fish the numerous bays around the peninsula's deeply indented coastline, especially during summer holidays.

Slooten and Dawson did a more detailed survey over 1984 to 1988 in the waters of Pegasus Bay, Banks Peninsula, and the Canterbury Bight, which showed incidental catches of between 26 and 90 Hector's dolphin each year. The numbers killed in commercial set-nets declined over the period, but the number caught in amateur nets increased. Because not all catches were reported, the actual numbers caught were probably even higher. Eighty-seven per cent of entanglement deaths occurred within 10 km (5 nautical miles) of the shore, and 60 per cent occurred within 2 km (one nautical mile). Over the period of study, 228 dolphins were reliably reported to have drowned in set-nets, out of a total population estimated in 1984 at 740.

Because Hector's dolphins cannot hold their breath for long and dives rarely exceed 2 minutes (compared with up to 8 minutes for a bottlenose dolphin), entanglement in a set-net is usually fatal. Slooten and Dawson found that many of the animals brought in to them were young animals, perhaps inexperienced in the use of their sonar. They discovered that almost all the reported drownings of dolphins occurred between November and February, when commercial fishermen bring their nets closer to shore, following the breeding dogfish and elephant fish. Although Hector's dolphins do not feed extensively on commercial fish species, they, too, move into the sheltered waters of the peninsula's bays to breed during the summer.

In years gone by, the impact of set-nets on the dolphins may have been even more serious. Of the 60 or so gill-net vessels which had worked around the peninsula in the late 1970s, only half a dozen remained by 1986. The introduction of quotas to regulate the commercial fish catch had removed a substantial number of set-netters from the industry. Because so little work had been carried out on Hector's dolphin before Slooten and Dawson began their studies, it is impossible to even guess at the number of dolphins which had been annually killed before 1984. Given the previous level of set-net effort, however, the population was probably originally much larger, and had been on the decrease for many years, at least since the rapid expansion of set-net use in the mid 1970s.

Slooten's work showed that female Hector's dolphins begin breeding between 7 and 9 years of age, and rarely live longer than 18 years. They produce a single calf once every 2 or 3 years. Even under the most favourable conditions, therefore, a female is unlikely to produce more than five calves in a lifetime, with three probably being a more realistic average. As the studies continued, it became increasingly obvious that the dolphins could not withstand the high losses they were suffering.

This slow breeding pattern is typical of small dolphins and porpoises. Jay Barlow of the US discovered that for the vaquita, new births into the population each year almost exactly balanced the losses through natural mortality. Like Hector's dolphin, the vaquita is incidentally caught in a gill-net fishery, and is unable to replace the losses through increased rates of reproduction.

Based on the data on incidental catch provided to Stephen Dawson, Canterbury University experts in population biology and mathematics calculated the likely effect of gill-netting on Hector's dolphin. Because so many of the drowned Banks Peninsula dolphins were young animals, the local dolphin population was predicted to continue to decline for many years, even if all set-net entanglements were stopped, simply because fewer dolphins would reach breeding age.

The New Zealand Government's Department of Conservation therefore proposed the introduction of restrictions on the use of set-nets around Banks Peninsula, through the use of an Act of Parliament which most New Zealanders had probably never heard of.

The Marine Mammals Protection Act was passed in New Zealand in 1978, and reflected a growing public awareness of the need to provide for the conservation of the country's marine mammals, which had been ruthlessly slaughtered during both the nineteenth and twentieth centuries. Section 22 of the Act provided for the establishment of marine mammal sanctuaries. This power had never been previously used, but became a key element in the plan to save Hector's dolphin through the establishment of a marine mammal sanctuary around Banks Peninsula. The proposed sanctuary area extended 7 km (4 miles) offshore, and covered an area of some 1140 square km (500 square miles).

When the Conservation Department proposed the establishment of the sanctuary in its discussion document, the public response was overwhelmingly favourable. An astonishing 6400 replies were received, more than 90 per cent of them supporting the creation of the sanctuary, while 80 per cent wanted a total or seasonal ban on set-netting within the sanctuary area. Included in this number were Martin Holdgate, Director-General of IUCN, and Professor David Gaskin, world expert on marine mammals. Gaskin, who is convinced that modern monofilament gill-nets have caused serious declines in dolphin and porpoise populations worldwide, is convinced that coastal porpoise and dolphin species are in decline everywhere, and is alarmed at the situation.

He believes the set-net or gill-net to be a devastating piece of equipment, and in a "first-world" country sees no excuse to continue fishing in this manner: "The counter-arguments of a handful of fishermen . . . not representative of the industry . . . should not be given any particular weight. In no way do they have a mandate to wipe out a whole stock and possibly a whole species simply for their convenience in carrying on with an unsophisticated fishing method."

The Minister of Conservation, Helen Clark, established the sanctuary one week before Christmas 1988. All commercial netting was prohibited within the sanctuary, and a ban was imposed on the use of all set-nets within the sanctuary during the months of November to February, thus enormously reducing recreational set-net use. The Department of Conservation estimated that 60–80 per cent of the dolphin mortalities of the previous 4 years could have been avoided by such restrictions.

Reaction to the establishment of the sanctuary was mixed. Conservation groups hailed the decision as enlightened, and there was little criticism from the fishing industry. However, local amateur fishers were outraged. Many felt that to be denied the use of a fishing net for 4 months each year was the removal of a fundamental human right. Slooten and Dawson were accused of fabricating their data, and of failing to count dolphins accurately.

The controversy created by the research suddenly put Hector's dolphin firmly in the public eye. Before the study began, few people knew about the dolphin, but the upsurge in public interest prompted many locals to claim that they were seeing more dolphins recently than ever before, whereas in fact they had probably just taken greater notice of something that had always been there. Others agreed with the idea of a sanctuary, but suggested that it should be situated somewhere else where there would be no conflicts with recreational fishing, prompting Steve Dawson to draw the analogy of "putting a plaster on your bum to treat a boil on your forehead."

After a few months, the controversy settled down, and the Department of Conservation announced a 3-year research programme to provide the answers to key questions about the status of the Banks Peninsula population of Hector's dolphin. The programme, which involves aerial surveys, DNA-fingerprinting, and photo-identification, will be a joint research effort between New Zealand and US scientists. At the conclusion of the programme, the Minister of Conservation will reassess the regulations required to provide protection for the down-under dolphin.

The Hector's story may have a happy ending, as the establishment of the marine mammal sanctuary should greatly reduce the rates of entanglement. Hector's dolphins are however still exposed to the hazard of set-net and, to a far lesser extent, trawl nets throughout the rest of their range in New Zealand. Also, the levels of pesticide residues and heavy metals in their tissues are high, as might be expected in animals with a coastal habitat. There is hope for Hector's, but it has certainly been saved from fishing nets at the last hour, and will need all the protection and help it can get if it is to survive through the next century.

**"Whatever we do or don't do, our children will have to live with."**
*Steve Dawson and Elizabeth Slooten, University of Canterbury, New Zealand*

*Hector's dolphin is a tiny (less than 1.5 metres) inshore-dwelling species found only in New Zealand. The total population now numbers only 3–4000, and the species is under threat from coastal gill-nets.* Steve Dawson

**Above**: A young Hector's dolphin entangled and drowned in a gill-net. Until the first major study of Hector's dolphin in the wild was carried out in the 1980s, nobody realised that a significant percentage of the total population was being killed like this each year. Steve Dawson

**Opposite**: A wild and free Hector's dolphin. The New Zealand government has now established a sanctuary to try and protect this endangered species. Steve Dawson

**Left**: Hector's dolphin killed in a gill-net, with the net marks visible around its neck. Because these small dolphins cannot hold their breath for long, entanglement in nets is usually fatal. Steve Dawson

"At the time we were theoretically tree shrews, whales were completely developed, and so were dolphins." (John Lilly)  Bob Talbot

# 11: POISONED WATERS

Small cetaceans face many threats through the loss of their habitat.
Industrial poisons, oil spills, and an increasing amount of modern
plastic debris foul the seas and rivers in which cetaceans live, while
pollution, hydro-electric dams, and forest clearance destroy the
specialised habitats of river dolphins.

## TOXIC INDUSTRIAL WASTES

For decades, the major industrial nations have used coastal seas as the
dumping ground and receptacle for a wide range of industrial and
agricultural toxins and waste products. Many dolphins and porpoises
are particularly vulnerable to these poisons, because of both their
coastal habitat and their position at the top of the food chain. The most
toxic residues from industrial society are rarely successfully neutralised
or excreted by living organisms, and they tend to be increasingly
concentrated in animal tissues as they are passed up the food chain.
Top predators, such as toothed whales and dolphins, can accumulate
large quantities in their tissues if they keep eating contaminated prey.

Small cetaceans are additionally vulnerable because their bodies
contain large volumes of fat and blubber. Chlorinated hydrocarbons,
which are some of the most persistent and environmentally damaging
of the industrial chemicals, and the industrial organochlorides known
as polychlorinated biphenyls (PCBs), are particularly soluble in fatty
tissues. Arctic and tropical cetaceans are relatively free from
chlorinated hydrocarbons, but those from temperate waters, especially
industrialised coastal waters, are often heavily contaminated.

## BELEAGUERED BELUGAS OF
## THE ST LAWRENCE RIVER

A century ago, as many as 5000 belugas or white whales lived in the St
Lawrence River in eastern Canada. Now the river has become so heavily
polluted with toxic industrial wastes that the belugas are among the
most contaminated mammals in the world. In fact, they are so
contaminated with PCBs alone that, under Canadian law, their corpses
must be treated as toxic waste to keep the poisonous chemical from
returning to the environment. The level of PCBs in belugas has been
measured as high as 1725 parts per million (ppm). Fish are judged to be
unfit for human consumption at just 2 ppm. The belugas of the St
Lawrence may now number only 400, and this local population is almost
certainly doomed to extinction.

The beluga is closely related to the narwhal, and both are found
mainly in the cold northern waters of Canada, Alaska, and the USSR.
Belugas can be found in all shallow waters, rivers, and estuaries of the
Arctic, and seem to be limited only by temperatures higher than 15°C
(60°F). A rotund species, they are striking for their creamy white colour
and remarkable range of sounds that can be clearly heard above the
surface of the water. These range from squeals – attributed by early
mariners to "sea canaries" – to a beautiful bell-like tone that is unique
among cetaceans.

When they were plentiful in the St Lawrence, the belugas were often
blamed for depleting fish stocks, and the Canadian government for

PCBs, although no longer produced,
were for 50 years widely used in
industry – for example as cooling
and insulating fluids and in the
manufacture of plastics, adhesives,
and lubricants. They are usually
colourless or pale yellow liquids,
and are fire resistant, stable,
soluble in fat, and highly toxic.
Because of their stability, they are
hard to dispose of and are
persistent environmental
contaminants. They can remain for
many years in cold and hostile
environments while retaining their
toxicity, and they have a tendency
to remain in living organisms. They
are carcinogenic and cause
infertility in many species. Almost
all PCBs are believed to enter the
oceans via the atmosphere,
enabling even the most remote
parts of the globe to become
contaminated. More than a billion
kilograms of PCBs were probably
produced, and a third of this is
believed to have leaked into the
environment because of careless
disposal. According to Joseph
Cummins of the University of
London, Ontario, the liberation of
only a small proportion of the
remaining PCBs would spell
disaster for marine mammals.

The St Lawrence River drains the Great Lakes, and both Canadian and US industries have been pouring toxic wastes into the lake and river system for decades, creating an increasingly lethal environment for the beluga. Their river habitat east of Quebec city has become a chemical soup of pollutants which probably causes a failure of their immune system or leads to a variety of other diseases such as bladder and other cancers, hepatitis, and perforated ulcers. Autopsies have identified at least 24 different contaminants in their bodies.

Simple laboratory tests were able to show the acutely toxic effects of large doses of organochlorines, but it took years for high concentrations to accumulate in belugas that had consumed large quantities of lightly-contaminated food. The stability of the organochlorines, an advantage in their industrial applications, ensured that they were not broken down in the natural environment. By the time the routine disposal of organochlorines was recognised to be a hazard, major consumers in many ecosystems, such as the belugas of the St Lawrence, were already heavily contaminated. The concentrations of DDT and PCB residues reported in many studies of dolphin and porpoise tissues have been shown experimentally to cause lowered fertility and premature births in both seals and sealions. Exposure to PCBs can result in failure of the body's immune system. DDT has been responsible for drastic population declines of many birds of prey, including fish-eating birds such as pelicans. Small cetaceans would probably not fare better than birds after exposure to excessive quantities of organochlorines. Indeed dolphins and porpoises may be particularly vulnerable because they apparently have a lower capacity for PCB degradation than birds.

many years paid a bounty for each whale killed. During the Second World War, trainee fighter pilots used them for target practice, and as recently as 1968, they were still being hunted for sport. Now PCBs and other industrial pollutants are killing off the beluga.

Ironically, at the eleventh hour the plight of the belugas has been given a boost by the success of whale-watching cruises in the St Lawrence. Public pressure on the Canadian and Quebec governments has resulted in the pledge of more than 2.4 billion dollars over the next 10 years to clean up the St Lawrence and create a marine sanctuary for the remaining belugas.

Much of the credit for the remarkable change in the attitudes of the Canadian public towards the St Lawrence belugas must go to ecologist Leone Pippard, commonly known as Our Lady of the White Whales. It was her solitary research and activism during the 1970s which alerted the world to the fact that despite the end of large-scale hunting in the 1950s, numbers had continued to decline, and the whales were on the verge of extinction.

In 1979, the Canadian government accorded protection status to the St Lawrence beluga population. During the same year, the first whale-watching vessel on the St Lawrence attracted only a handful of supporters, but a decade later, the numbers have swelled to over 60,000 tourists a year, with revenues from whale-watching now approaching 2 million dollars annually. Ironically, tour operators are strictly forbidden from seeking out belugas, because they are an endangered species, but the beluga has nevertheless become a powerful symbol of ecological neglect for those who have experienced the 3-hour cruises, complete with detailed lectures about the animal's plight.

Even after they had received total protection status, beluga numbers in the St Lawrence continued to decline, and autopsies of dead whales during the 1980s revealed astonishing levels of toxic chemicals – in particular organochlorines such as PCBs, the insecticides DDT and mirex, and dioxin.

When whales eat contaminated prey, organochlorines go first to the digestive system, and are then deposited in fatty tissues. Because they cannot generally be metabolised or excreted, organochlorines tend to accumulate gradually in the blubber, which in adult belugas accounts for 35 per cent of the body weight. Conventional scientific wisdom has held that whales are relatively immune from the effects of toxic chemicals, because such contaminants were thought to be safely stored in the blubber, a tissue considered to be fairly inert.

Pierre Beland and Daniel Martineau were members of a research team which showed that the concept of blubber as an inert tissue was incorrect – the ratios of contaminants in samples from over 70 autopsied belugas has shown that toxins are continually exchanged between various tissues.

Beland and Martineau also discovered that male belugas were much more contaminated than females, and that year-old calves were, strangely, often the most contaminated of all. However, female belugas, who bear a single calf every three years, have a mechanism for unloading organochlorines. Small amounts of contaminants are transferred from mother to foetus, but much greater quantities are passed to the suckling young through her milk. Whale milk is very rich in fats, making it an ideal carrier of organochlorines.

The massive contamination in the animals autopsied in recent years provides little cause for optimism. By the time the St Lawrence River is restored to health, the belugas will probably be gone. The sad fate of the St Lawrence belugas epitomises the problems faced by small cetaceans on an increasingly polluted planet. In many ways, the St Lawrence belugas have provided a perfect opportunity for scientists to study the effects of contaminants on a wild whale population, since they are isolated from other groups, and live in a river system known to be contaminated. Sometime in the future belugas will return to a clean St Lawrence River, either naturally or by a programme of capture and release from other wild populations.

## COASTAL CETACEANS SUFFER THE MOST FROM TOXIC WASTES

In the 1970s a study of dolphin and porpoise tissues, from several locations throughout the Pacific, demonstrated that coastal dolphins and porpoises are the most susceptible to accumulating toxic waste, especially those whose habitat is close to industrial discharges or run-off of agricultural chemicals.

California is the major industrial polluter of the eastern Pacific seaboard. The oceanic input of PCBs from five southern California sewage treatment plants was estimated at nearly 200 tonnes per year in 1972. One Los Angeles pesticide manufacturer alone was responsible for a continuous discharge of DDT at sewer outfalls for 20 years, dumping almost 250 kg (550 lb) per day into the ocean. Not surprisingly, mean concentrations of DDT and related compounds were up to seven times higher in the blubber of male common dolphins from the southern California area than from any species sampled elsewhere in the Pacific, including Japan. PCB residues in the blubber of the California bottlenose dolphin also exceeded previously published concentrations for cetaceans from all other parts of the world, except perhaps the Mediterranean coast of France, which have been reported to have a maximum concentration of over 2500 ppm.

The true effect on wild dolphin populations of prolonged exposure to chemical pollutants is hard to measure. Because much of a dolphin's life is spent beyond the range of human observation, such basic characteristics as reproductive rates and life expectancy are much harder to measure than with birds and land mammals. However, there is abundant anecdotal evidence of the effects of chemical pollution on the populations of small cetaceans inhabiting industrialised areas. Until the nineteenth century, for example, bottlenose dolphins occurred in all the major estuaries in Britain, including the Thames and the Humber. Now they can be found only in the Moray Firth in Scotland. Whether the dolphins' population has declined or whether they simply avoid the more contaminated areas and have moved to remoter regions is not clear. The harbour porpoise, common in the North Sea until the 1930s, has now disappeared from the Thames estuary, Firth of Forth, Firth of Tay, the Clyde, Tyne, Tees, and Mersey rivers, and the Bristol Channel.

In areas with only restricted opportunities for mixing and dilution of industrial wastes, such as the Baltic Sea, contamination of marine mammals is an especially pressing problem. The common seals of the Wadden Sea vie with the St Lawrence belugas and Mediterranean bottlenose dolphins for the dubious distinction of the world's most PCB-contaminated animal. Almost 80 per cent of the female seals in the Baltic are known to be sterile, primarily as a result of PCB poisoning, and by the year 2000, grey seals in the Baltic may well have become extinct.

DDT and PCB levels in the blubber of a few porpoises from eastern Scotland analysed in 1967 were considerably higher than in seals from the same area. A similar result has been found in the Gulf of St Lawrence in Canada.

# POLLUTION MAY CAUSE MASSIVE DIE-OFFS

At low levels of contamination, organochlorines such as PCBs may lower an animal's resistance to infection, and can be the cause of mass deaths. During January 1980, for example, over 500 bottlenose dolphins were washed up on the Atlantic coast of France. No obvious cause of death was found, but all the dolphins were heavily contaminated with PCBs.

In another incident, during the summer of 1987, hundreds of dead and dying bottlenose dolphins were washed ashore on beaches of the East Coast of the US, from New Jersey to Florida. In the following 18 months, more than 750 emaciated dolphin bodies were washed ashore, although US officials now estimate that as many as 3000 dolphins may have died with similar symptoms. Most of the dolphins that were washed up had died from internal haemorrhaging. They had fluid in their lungs, enlarged spleens, bronchial pneumonia, and their skin peeled off like plastic food wrap. Their immune systems had apparently broken down. According to Greenpeace biologists, the dolphins all had high levels of PCBs in their tissues, although the official report blamed their death on poisonous algae in their fish prey.

Coastal cetaceans not only pick up chlorinated hydrocarbons, but also accumulate other industrial pollutants such as heavy metals. Many industrial processes discharge to the environment such metals as zinc, copper, cadmium and, most dangerous of all, mercury. Many governments are very strict about imposing restrictions on the importation of foodstuffs which contain excessive concentrations of heavy metals. Japan in particular has been particularly conscious of the devastating effect of mercury poisoning after hundreds of Japanese died or were permanently crippled in the 1950s after exposure to mercury-contaminated fish. The mercury had been discharged from a local chemical plant.

Surveys of dolphin tissues for mercury carried out in 1978 by Japanese scientists showed very high levels of mercury in local dolphins. The highest rating was for the bottlenose dolphin, which had a mercury content as much as 130 times the maximum permitted level for human consumption (0.5 ppm). For the striped dolphin, until recently the most commonly eaten species in Japan, the mean mercury level was 12 times the maximum allowable level.

"There are clear signs that the oceans are dying. And when the oceans die, forget it. We are gone."
*Leone Pippard,*
*Our Lady of the White Whales*

# PLASTICS AND THE MARINE DEBRIS PERIL

Plastic debris is filling up our oceans and is another modern peril that is taking its toll on dolphins and other marine mammals. Lost or deliberately discarded fishing nets pose the biggest threat, but seemingly more innocent items like plastic bags, plastic pellets, and polypropylene packing tape can also be killers of wildlife.

Small whales and dolphins are not only caught in nets that are actively fishing, but also in set-nets that break away from their anchors, lost or discarded trawl nets, and, in particular, lost portions of the enormous oceanic drift-nets, which become "ghost nets" that float in the ocean and continue to catch fish and other marine life. These drifting nets of thin monofilament nylon may each be up to 50 km (31 miles) in length, and portions are inevitably lost in bad weather. In the North Pacific Ocean the 1987-88 driftnet fleet of roughly 1600 Taiwanese, Japanese, and Korean vessels was estimated to deploy 50,000 km (31,000 miles) of net each night for several months each year. According to official Japanese government estimates, 0.2 per cent of the nets set each night are not recovered, although the rate of loss is probably much higher, perhaps as much as 2 per cent. Even the official

According to a US National Academy of Sciences study in 1975, the world's fishing vessels each year dump more than 24,000 tonnes of plastic packaging material and lose an additional 135,000 tonnes of plastic nets, lines and buoys. Several thousand kilometres of fish netting is lost or discarded at sea annually. Each day the world's merchant shipping fleet, by one reliable estimate made in 1982, discards 639,000 plastic containers into the sea.

Japanese estimates would result in 1100 km (690 miles) of netting being released into the North Pacific each year, with a life expectancy measured in decades, if not centuries. These remnants may be rolled into balls of netting and sink, or may continue to catch fish, sea birds and marine mammals as they drift in the ocean currents, sinking with the weight of entangled wildlife, only to rise towards the surface again as the bodies decompose. One segment of drift-net recovered from the Alaskan coastline was 1.5 km (1 mile) long and contained 99 dead sea birds, over 200 dead salmon and a seal skull.

The recent rapid expansion of Asian drift-net fleets into the South Pacific and Tasman Sea has raised fears of similar problems of entanglement of marine mammals in plastic netting lost or discarded in these areas.

The attitude to the disposal of plastics varies greatly among countries. Korean skippers, for example, must pass an examination in plastics disposal before they are commissioned, and must keep a daily log to ensure that all plastic rubbish has been kept on board. Observers frequently report that Japanese, Taiwanese, and Korean fishermen make every effort to retrieve net fragments for recycling. Even with this care, however, so great are the quantities of drift-net in use that the loss of some of the millions of kilometres of netting deployed each year is inevitable.

Other forms of plastics also hold hazards for small cetaceans. Plastic bags may be lethal when swallowed in mistake for food. Minke whales, sperm whales, and killer whales have all been reported stranded on Australian and New Zealand beaches with their stomachs or throats full of plastic bags or sheets. Discarded or lost fishing line and plastic strapping bands used in the fishing industry can form lethal collars for both dolphins and seals. Once around a young marine mammal's neck, the plastic collar will slowly cut deeper into the animal's flesh as it grows, until the animal is throttled or dies of starvation or infection.

# NOISE

Noise generated by industrial activity and boat traffic is transmitted especially well under water. The noise from oil rigs is within the frequency range of dolphin vocalisations and can be detected from a distance of 80 km (50 miles) with hydrophones. Noises of such intensity may seriously affect the ability of cetaceans to communicate and echolocate, especially in cold polar waters where ice cover reflects much underwater noise back from the surface. Migrating bowhead whales are reported to give drilling ships in the Beaufort Sea a wide berth on their migrations. Scientists report that the inner ears of Weddell seals in McMurdo Sound, Antarctica, have been damaged by seismic blasts.

# OIL

Little is known of the general effects of oil on the distribution of small cetaceans. When large quantities of oil are released after the break-up of a tanker, for example, sea birds appear to be more visibly affected than the smooth-skinned dolphins, possibly because cetaceans can choose to swim away from oil slicks, and do not have to keep returning through slicks to nesting sites on shore.

The effects of oil pollution on marine mammals are more severe in colder waters, not only because of the much longer time required for the oil to break down, but also because concentrations of cetaceans and other marine mammals are often larger in polar waters.

**Commercial gill-net fisheries should be phased out wherever suitable alternative techniques are available. If they are not, monofilament nets must be replaced by biodegradable multifilament nets made out of a material like cotton, which are detectable by dolphin sonar. More research should be carried out into how to modify nets so that dolphins are warned to keep clear.**

**The wildlife toll exacted by lost and abandoned fishing gear is staggering. According to an estimate by the Entanglement Network, a coalition of 18 environmental groups in Washington, DC, lost or discarded plastic is killing up to 2 million sea birds and 100,000 marine mammals each year.**

**The proposal to use nuclear-powered icebreaking supertankers (the Arctic Pilot project) to transport oil and gas from the Canadian Arctic fortunately never proceeded past the planning stage. Their noise would have undoubtedly caused enormous damage to the sensitive hearing of marine mammals. Beluga whales emit distress calls when even a conventional icebreaker is 80 km (50 miles) away, and flee when such vessels approach within 40 km (25 miles).**

Conservationists have for many years been predicting the catastrophic consequences of a major oil spill in Arctic or Antarctic seas, and in early 1989, their worst fears were realised. The Argentine resupply and tourist ship *Bahia Paraiso* ran aground near major penguin rookeries in the Antarctic Peninsula, just offshore from the US research base of Palmer Station. The vessel was carrying one million litres (more than a quarter of a million US gallons) of oil, diesel, jet fuel, and compressed gas. A year later, the vessel was still firmly aground. Thousands of birds, particularly skuas and their chicks, died from exposure to the spilt fuel, and the toll on seals and small whales is unkown.

Yet the *Bahia Paraiso* tragedy seemed of little consequence compared with the disaster which occurred in northern polar waters only weeks later. The 350-metre (1140-foot) supertanker *Exxon Valdez* left the Alaskan oil terminal port of Valdez on the night of 24 March, loaded with 230 million litres (61 million US gal) of crude oil. Within an hour and a half, the *Exxon Valdez* had eluded the coastguard radar tracking system and plunged at full speed on to the rocks of Bligh Reef, rupturing eight cargo holds, each big enough to house a 15-storey building.

The environmental consequences of the accident, which oil companies described during legal hearings in the 1970s as a "one in a million" possibility, have been catastrophic. Hundreds of kilometers of coastline were covered with a thick layer of oil 15–20 cm (6–8 inches) thick, with a mousse-like consistency. The effects on small cetaceans are unknown, but 10 gray whales were found dead on Alaskan beaches in May. The whales were coated with oil, picked up when they entered Alaskan waters on their summer migration from Mexico and California, to feed in the rich northern waters.

Prince William Sound appears ruined as a healthy marine environment for years, if not decades. As even the remotest parts of the earth are threatened by modern industrial society, the future for not only dolphins but for all marine wildlife looks increasingly insecure.

## ATMOSPHERIC POLLUTION

Adding to the problems caused by what is being dumped into the seas and waterways of the world are the profound and unpredictable consequences of atmospheric pollution. The combination of global warming and the increasing damage to the ozone layer will undoubtedly have profound effects on ocean productivity, currents and upwellings and will result in changes in the abundance and distribution of many marine species. Most threatening for the marine ecosystem is the exposure to increased ultra-violet radiation through the depletion of the ozone layer.

In an experiment carried out at Palmer Station on the Antarctic Peninsula in 1989, microscopic floating ocean plants (phytoplankton) were taken from the nearby bay and brought into the laboratory, where they were subjected to levels of ultra-violet radiation estimated to be equivalent to the amount of ultra-violet being transmitted through the ozone hole which has been developing in Antarctica each spring in recent years. The plant's production dived, in some cases to as little as one-eighth of the normal rate.

Since then, the ozone hole in Antarctica has continued to grow each year, with increasingly grave potential consequences for photosynthesis in the southern ocean. In 1992, the International Whaling Commission adopted a resolution which directed the IWC's Scientific Committee to consider each year the latest research into the effects of ozone depletion on whales in the Antarctic Ocean.

# 12: DOLPHINS AND WHALES IN CAPTIVITY

The human desire to hold wild animals in captivity has raised ethical questions over the thousands of years that we have been capturing and caging all manner of creatures for study and entertainment. Dolphins managed to largely escape such treatment until recently, but now their high intelligence, playful friendly natures, and general popular appeal, have made them much in demand for research studies, oceanaria and marinelands, and commercial tourist operations.

Dolphins were first put on public display in the 1860s, at London's Westminster Aquarium. Although they were popular exhibits at this and other aquaria, their life expectancy in captivity proved to be very short, and numerous attempts in both Europe and the USA over the subsequent 80 years failed to improve survival rates.

Then in 1938 scientific study of dolphins became popular, and most of the dolphins captured at this time were headed for research establishments. Dolphins were often dreadfully tortured in the name of science. United States neurologist Dr John Lilly, a pioneer of research into dolphin intelligence and consciousness, inserted electrodes into the brains of living dolphins, driving holes into their skulls (thought to be every bit as sensitive as a human skull) with a carpenter's hammer. John Lilly did much to inspire human appreciation of dolphin intelligence, but at such high cost to dolphins that he eventually closed down his dolphin research institute and belatedly regretted the concentration camp he had created there. However, the world's scientific community is still full of zeal for dolphin research and is quite prepared to kill to prove its theories. In one of many examples, a joint team from the University of California and the Medical University in Tokyo in 1968 killed 29 dolphins to investigate sound production and noise conduction.

As the biologists made their discoveries about dolphin behaviour, much of this knowledge began to be taken up by trainers in the dolphin entertainment trade. Dolphins were taught to perform tricks like throwing and catching balls, leaping through hoops and responding to human communication. Specialised dolphinaria opened throughout the United States in the 1950s, and the public flocked to see the dolphin shows. The television programme "Flipper" introduced the world to a clever friendly dolphin with a grinning face and human attributes and he won many hearts. By 1991, captive dolphins had become a billion dollar a year industry in the US alone. The major exhibitor, Sea World, which keeps 85 captive dolphins, attracted ten million paying customers through the turnstiles of its marine parks in Florida, Texas, Ohio and California.

The International Whaling Commission (IWC) reported in 1987 that over the previous 30 years, 4580 small cetaceans were captured alive for display purposes. Over half were bottlenose dolphins, but some much rarer species, such as the Amazon River dolphin were also taken. This figure doesn't include those dolphins who didn't make it alive to the tanks. Records of California dolphinaria show that in 1975, 40 per cent of their cetaceans died during capture, and this figure is probably typical of many other dolphin capture operations.

Facilities for captive dolphins vary enormously. In primitive circus-type enterprises, animals may be kept permanently in a small tank and asked to perform the same tasks repeatedly for spectators. Sanitation

Many newer (or more enlightened) aquariums are giving up captive dolphins entirely. The Cousteau Society has even developed an Ocean Park in Paris with no live animals and not a drop of water. The display features interactive videos, a wide-screen film of the underwater world and a walk through the inside of a life-size model of a 27-m (90-ft) blue whale.

Supplying live cetaceans is now a highly specialised job. Most of the captures are made with seine nets, except in Japan where dolphins supplied for display are usually those spared from slaughter after a successful drive. A more bizarre method of capture is used for the long-suffering beluga, whose hunters manoeuvre small boats in among a pod (small herd), then leap on to the whales' backs and lasso them. These "beluga busters" then ride them until exhausted. The animals often go into a state of shock or even die.

**Rare river dolphins have died soon after delivery to aquaria in Tokyo, Florida and California. The Vancouver aquarium has tried on several occasions over the past 20 years to be the first in Canada to successfully display the rare one-horned narwhal – seven animals have been captured but none has lived for very long.**

and hygiene are often of a low standard or virtually non-existent, and the mortality rates are high, with many animals dying soon after capture. Many of the shoddiest institutions in the western world closed down in the 1980s, but in places like Taiwan they still continue. The best establishments, which are still not the majority, offer separate performing and living quarters, trained veterinarians, and plenty of skilled trainers to keep the dolphins amused and healthy. Some are incredibly expensive, such as the US$120 million "Tropical World" being developed high in the Swiss Alps, where killer whales and dolphins will perform under a huge dome beneath the snow-capped peaks.

The problems and risks for dolphins held in captivity are many. Poor hygiene, sanitation and feeding cause mortality in the cheaper institutions. In poorly supervised situations, dolphins frequently choke to death on objects thrown to them by the public, and rugby balls, gloves, camera holders and tin cans have all been found in the stomachs of dead animals. Even in the better-equipped and staffed facilities, many small cetaceans cannot adjust to life in captivity. The most lavish care cannot compensate for the huge restrictions placed on an animal used to travelling over thousands of miles of ocean and waterway, and living and communicating in large groups. High stress levels and boredom can lead to physical illness and death.

Scientists have recently discovered that captive dolphins can suffer severe stress from being observed by thousands of humans each day. When the National Aquarium in Baltimore constructed a multi-million dollar tank, three bottlenose dolphins were acquired for the opening in 1981. Crowds of as many 1000 people per hour flocked to see the dolphins, but after only 50 days, the animals became ill and were flown back to the Dolphin Research Centre in Florida, where gastro-intestinal ulcers were diagnosed.

Having invested so much money in developing the exhibit, aquarium staff were anxious to discover what had gone wrong. Extensive research showed that the dolphins were scared by the noise of the crowds, but the tank was too small to allow them to retreat to a distance where they felt more at ease. To make matters worse, in fleeing from the crowds, the dolphins congregated in a spot where the noise from the tank's pumps was loudest, and they were more unhappy than ever.

Some species, such as the rare one-horned narwhal, and many of the river dolphins do not seem to be able to survive captivity. Other individuals commit suicide under the duress of captivity. When a dolphinarium in the Netherlands took possession of a rare beaked whale, it kept throwing itself against the tank wall until it broke its beak and died. The frustrations of captivity can also drive cetaceans to uncharacteristic violence and aggression.

A recent trend in the dolphin entertainment business is the development of travelling dolphin shows, where smiling cetaceans perform tricks in improvised pools and are touted around popular holiday resorts and large towns. Sometimes the shows are leased to large resort hotels which provide performing dolphins as part of the entertainment laid on for guests. In a recent unsavoury incident, two bottlenose dolphins called Lemo and Nemo were confined to the pool of the Meridien Hotel in Cairo for a year. The animals, originally caught off Guatemala, were owned by a Swiss dolphin entrepreneur, Bruno Lienhardt, who had been contracted by the management to run the dolphin show for one year in the hotel's pool by the Nile River. One of the dolphins had been part of Lienhardt's shows at the Moulin Rouge in Paris.

The legal wrangling and publicity resulting from the suffering the dolphins experienced in the Meridien Hotel pool turned the attention of animal rights activists towards the increasing trend for exhibiting dolphins in hotels and allowing humans to swim with captive dolphins.

*"... and Venus among the fishes skips and is a she-dolphin, she is the gay, delighted porpoise sporting with love and the sea." (D.H. Lawrence)* Bob Talbot

*Right: Belugas, or white whales, are still being hunted for food in the Arctic. In the St Lawrence River, Canada, pollution has already sealed their fate by rendering them sterile. So badly are they contaminated that dead belugas are treated as toxic waste. Elsewhere, many belugas are also captured alive for display, despite strong opposition from conservationists.* Sean R. Whyte/ WDCS

*Below and opposite: Orca bulls in Puget Sound, Washington.* Bob Talbot

A family group of orcas in the wild. Orcas regularly travel over 100 kilometres a day – by contrast, in an oceanarium they are confined in tanks less than 60 metres long. Bob Talbot

*Above*: Leaping white-sided dolphins perform with a false killer whale at Sea World, Orlando, Florida. Sean R. Whyte/WDCS

*Opposite*: Spotted dolphins. "There is a widening sense that we need the beasts of the sea just as they are – alive and free." (Victor B. Scheffer)  Bob Talbot

*Left*: Although these white-sided dolphins bring delight to human spectactors, the consequences are often dire for dolphins kept in captivity. Even in the best-equipped facilities, life expectancy is significantly reduced.  Sean R Whyte/WDCS

*Above*: Sex and play are a major part of the life of dolphins; cetaceans are among the few creatures apart from humans that mate when the female is not in season – an obvious sign of high social development. Bob Talbot

*Right*: Pygmy killer whales. James Watt

# ORCAS IN CAPTIVITY

The most commercially valuable cetacean species for display purposes is the killer whale, or orca. Far larger than dolphins (a fully grown male may be over 9 metres (30 feet) in length), the spectacular performing orcas can attract huge crowds, but require far more care and much larger facilities.

Up to 150 orcas have been captured for display, but most of these have died during or shortly after capture. Most of the early captures took place in Washington State, British Columbia, although Iceland has now become the world's main supplier of orcas. Three pods (small herds) in Puget Sound have dropped in numbers from 110 to approximately 75 animals as a result of the live captures. The effects on the social structure of the pods are not known.

In response to growing public opposition to the removal of orcas from the wild, Washington State prohibited any further live captures in 1976, which was also the time of the last capture from Canadian waters.

In Iceland, however, where they are considered a pest, orcas may still be taken. In fact, the export of orcas has become a lucrative trade. According to an article published in the London *Daily Express* in November 1989, orcas are such good crowd-pullers that Japanese aquaria will pay as much as UK£600,000 for a good specimen.

The capture and display of such large and active marine mammals as killer whales has been a major concern of numerous animal rights groups in the US for many years, but has become especially controversial recently with the involvement of the huge US publishing company Harcourt Brace Jovanovich (HBJ) in the orca display business. Soon after HBJ bought the Sea World marine park at San Diego, California, there were a series of increasingly serious incidents between trainers and whales. The most widely publicised incident took place in November 1987, when Orky, a mature bull orca weighing more than 5.5 tonnes, deliberately smashed into a trainer during a public performance, inflicting serious injuries.

Less than a year later, however, Orky was dead, having lost almost 2000 kg (4400 lb) (one-third of his body weight) during his 18 months at Sea World. The whale had been living in good health for the previous 16 years at Marineland in Palos Verdes, Southern California, but was transferred to San Diego when HBJ purchased and closed the rival theme park in January 1987.

Orky's longtime companion, Corky, was also transferred to the San Diego facility, and on 21 August 1989, she was involved in a dramatic incident which stirred a fresh wave of controversy over the ethics of keeping in a small tank animals which would normally swim as far as 150 km (95 miles) per day in the sea. Corky rammed a smaller 14-year-old female orca, Kandu, at full speed in front of a crowd of several thousand. The show's announcer, utterly unprepared for such an incident, continued with his bubblegum commentary as the water in Sea World's tank turned red and Kandu sank to the bottom. She bled to death within minutes, from a severed blood vessel in her fractured jaw. Sea World veterinarians said that the two female whales had rivalled for dominance since they first met 2 years earlier, when Orky and Corky were brought from Palos Verdes, and that the orcas had fought before the show, with Kandu attacking first. Eye witnesses thought that Kandu had been protecting her calf, Shamu, who had been born at Sea World 10 months earlier. Orky had fathered the calf in his healthier days, and many felt that Corky may have been settling an old jealousy score.

The dreadful publicity surrounding the death of Kandu brought an end to HBJ's short-lived expansion into the whale entertainment business. In September 1989, HBJ sold its four Sea World parks to brewing giant Anheuser-Busch (the makers of Budweiser beer), in a US$1.1 billion deal.

When the US$360 million Hyatt Regency Waikoloa Hotel on the coast of the island of Hawaii opened early in 1989, among the "entertainment staff" were eight bottlenose dolphins kept in an artificial lagoon which is attached to the hotel. As part of the fantasy theme of the hotel, which is the most expensive ever built, guests could pay US$55 to spend a half hour in the water with the dolphins.

For several months all went well as record numbers of wealthy hotel guests queued up to swim with the dolphins. Then two of the dolphins died within a month, both at night, without showing any prior symptoms. The deaths were a special worry for both the hotel and federal licensing authorities, because the "swim-with-dolphin" progamme had been touted as providing the best facilities and care that money could buy. The animals lived in a lagoon of 4000 square metres (4800 square yards), with conditions as close to their natural habitat as could be created, and the finest medical programme possible. Nobody knows what went wrong.

The publicity generated, and the popularity of the scheme with guests, are nevertheless encouraging other hotel promoters to plan similar operations. The developer of the Waikoloa resort has announced plans for 10 more "mega-resorts" across the US. Unless hotel developers are prepared to invest the substantial quantities of money required to provide adequate facilities and treatment for their captive dolphins, the premature death rate typical of the poorer oceanaria will undoubtedly be repeated. Hotel patrons may delight in swimming with the dolphins for an hour or two, but the dolphins are paying for this pleasure with their lives.

Four permitted commercial swim-with-dolphin operations were operating in the US during 1989, holding about 34 dolphins, and about 40,000 people were expected to swim with them. Federal permits for the facilities – Dolphins Plus, Theatre of the Sea, and the Dolphin Research Centre, all in Florida, and the Hyatt Waikoloa Resort in Hawaii – expired in March 1990, and the review process is certain to generate fierce debate. The state of Florida announced in January its official opposition to the renewal of permits to swim with dolphins in all three facilities in the Florida Keys.

The potential is obvious for commercial exploitation in the promotion of swim-with-dolphin programmes, particularly those planned for luxury hotels. Strong opposition from conservation and animal welfare groups was unable to prevent the US NMFS from granting a permit in September 1989 for the Las Vegas Mirage Hotel to display six dolphins, but stringent restrictions were set on the operation. No dolphins are to be taken from the wild. Only animals already in captivity can be displayed. No dolphin shows or swim-with-dolphin programmes are allowed. Appropriate sex ratios are to be maintained and public education programmes are to be developed. Conservationists hope that these restrictions will dissuade other hotels from seeking to develop new dolphin operations.

The standard argument for dolphinaria is that they are educational, and that they nurture an understanding and a sense of respect and awe for cetaceans that then serves to support the efforts of conservation groups to protect animals in the wild. Some swim-with-dolphin programmes may have a social value, such as at Dolphins Plus, in the Florida Keys, where volunteers supervise the pairing of autistic children with dolphins, and claim that the experience of playing with dolphins can have a profound effect on the children. The Dolphin Research Centre in Florida claims that public swim-with-dolphin programmes are essential to provide funding for research efforts and rescuing stranded animals, and point out that only three of the Centre's 17 dolphins have been captured from the wild when healthy – the majority have been brought in from strandings or accidents.

The social and educational value of dolphinaria may be true in many respects, but can also be a noble justification for what is essentially a commercial enterprise to make money for the owners. And dolphin performances are generally extremely banal, with trainers shaping the mammals' behaviour to fit around a script which is designed to entertain rather than inform the audience.

Many countries are now beginning to reassess the morality of keeping dolphins in captivity for public entertainment, and to impose more stringent standards of care. The six dolphinaria in Britain were heavily criticised in a report prepared by Dr Margaret Klinowska for the Department of the Environment in 1986. Among major criticisms were the small enclosures in which dolphins and killer whales have been kept. Klinowska recommended that all pools holding dolphins should be 7 metres (23 feet) deep, and those holding killer whales should be up to 15 metres (49 feet) deep. Although such dimensions would seem to be minimal in comparison with the natural lifestyle of these cetaceans, considerable opposition was expressed by the management of the dolphinaria.

In 1988, the Australian state of Victoria passed a law prohibiting the capture or display of dolphins within the sea and land under state jurisdiction. With increasingly stringent regulations coming in throughout the world, we can hope that only the best equipped and staffed marinelands will in future be allowed to display dolphins and whales. But even in well-equipped facilities, with skilled and caring trainers, many cetaceans pine, go crazy and die young.

A hopeful sign of change is the increasing popularity of trips to visit dolphins in the wild. All over the world whale and dolphin-watching cruises are allowing people to see and enjoy cetaceans in their natural environment, in ways that don't harm or trap these wild creatures. We can enjoy dolphins without having to keep them in a jail to do so.

**At Marineland in Napier, New Zealand, four common dolphins have been held in captivity in a large concrete tank for over a decade. They are allowed only a few playthings, one of which is a large brass bell by the side of the pool, which they can ring by tugging on a piece of rope. The melancholy sound of a bored dolphin repeatedly ringing the bell is one of the saddest of sounds. Perhaps it is a requiem for the millions that have died at human hands, and for those that continue to suffer from the relentless onslaught.**

**"I no longer want to run a concentration camp for my friends."**
*John Lilly, US neurologist*

## BELUGAS IN CAPTIVITY

Largely because of Leone Pippard's efforts to save the belugas of the St Lawrence River, public opinion in Canada has been swinging against the display of belugas in captivity, and especially against their export. In September 1989, Canadian Minister of Fisheries and Oceans, Tom Siddon, announced that a request from Shedd Oceanarium in Chicago to capture three belugas from Hudson Bay had been declined. Conservationists applauded the decision, but their joy was short-lived. A few weeks later, Siddon reversed his decision.

In order to beat the threat of lengthy litigation by environmental groups, which might have prevented the Oceanarium from opening on schedule, the Shedd team swiftly completed the captures, and two 400-kg (880-lb) animals were flown to the Point Defiance Aquarium in Tacoma, Washington State, a 9-hour journey in a small plane. Had they been prepared to wait for another couple of days, the weekend jet flight would have taken less than half the time.

On arrival at the Tacoma aquarium, the newly caught belugas were placed in a tank with three other white whales that had been living together in the same tank for 6 years. In August 1992, four belugas were transferred to the Shedd Oceanarium, but one month later two of them were dead. The World Society for the Protection of Animals (WSPA) was outraged, especially when they learnt that a Chicago judge had been allowed to take a 'thrill ride' on one of the whales after it had been caught with a rope in shallow water on the rocky shores of Hudson Bay.

Public opposition to the captive display of belugas has been increasing in Canada, and following representations from WSPA, Montreal's state-of-the-art ecological museum, Biodome, agreed in 1992 to forego its 12-year permit to capture and exhibit belugas.

## DEPROGRAMMING CAPTIVE DOLPHINS

Dolphins that have been held in captivity for any length of time need to be "de-programmed" before they can be confidently released back to the wild. The Oceanic Research and Communication Alliance (ORCA) has successfully rehabilitated two bottlenose dolphins which had been previously confined for 6 years in steel laboratory tanks as part of an unsuccessful language experiment carried out by John Lilly at Marine World in Redwood City, California. The dolphins, Joe and Rosie, were weaned from human dependency by trainer Richard O'Barry, who had trained the dolphins used in the television series "Flipper" during the 1960s, but it was a lengthy and expensive business.

Joe and Rosie were first taken to the Dolphin Research Center on Grassy Key, in the Florida Keys, where they lived in a fenced-off pen in the warm ocean waters, experiencing once again the rise and fall of the tides. O'Barry gradually introduced live fish into the pen, so that the dolphins could re-learn the art of capturing their prey. Initially, the trainer trimmed the tails of live snapper to slow them down, but as the dolphins became more adept, live mullet were flown in and tossed into the pen with tails intact.

In preparation for the move to their next home, a remote wildlife refuge on the southeast Atlantic Coast of the US, the underwater sounds of the refuge inhabitants were played to Joe and Rosie. The dolphins became accustomed to oysters opening and closing their shells, the movement of marsh grasses, and the strange new sounds of whitefish, flounder, and shrimp. The refuge had not only been selected for its abundant fish life, but also because several wild dolphin mothers and calves were frequently found there. This was especially important, because Rosie was pregnant, and would require the assistance of other female dolphins to successfully rear her calf.

In June 1987, Joe and Rosie were transported by helicopter to a large pen in the refuge, where after a further few months, the door to the pen was opened, and the dolphins swam free once more. The experiment seems to have been successful, judging by the regular reports of sightings of the distinctive marks freeze-branded on their dorsal fins. Ric O'Barry now runs The Dolphin Project, a watchdog group that monitors the treatment of marine mammals. He also offers a deprogramming service for returning captive dolphins to the wild, most recently retraining Brazil's last captive dolphin for release. O'Barry warns, however, that it isn't a cheap process — he estimates the price tag for reprogramming Joe and Rosie was US$150,000.

## BELUGA ON THE RUN

In 1991, a 5-m white whale briefly became an international media star for a few weeks when it turned up in the warm waters of the north Turkish coast near the town of Gerze. The whale was befriended by fishermen, who named it Aydin ('Brightness'), and fed it with fish. As perplexed biologists wondered how an arctic whale had found its way to the Black Sea, embarrassed Russian authorities admitted that Aydin had escaped from a 'biological research establishment' in Sevastopol, 800 km north of Gerze.

Although environmental groups offered to return the whale to its natural habitat or support its continued freedom in the Black Sea, the Turkish Government eventually succumbed to Russian demands and allowed Aydin to be recaptured and returned to captivity. Conservationists did not give up, however, and after extensive negotiations with Russian scientists, Ray Gravenor of the British Marine Life Rescue Association was given the go-ahead to rehabilitate Aydin for release to the wild in the Okhotsk Sea north of Japan. 'Brightness' is currently in training to be the first whale ever to be released from captivity. The future of up to 120 other dolphins and belugas in Russian military and scientific research establishments remains unclear.

## BALTIMORE AQUARIUM DOLPHIN CAPTURE
## WRANGLE – A TURNING POINT?

In Florida, conservationists and local residents have been increasingly concerned over the capture of dolphins from the coastal waters of the state for display or military conscription. Matters were brought to a head by the capture of two male bottlenose dolphins for the National Aquarium in Baltimore. The aquarium received a federal permit to capture six wild dolphins for its new US$35 million Marine Mammal Pavilion and hired Jay Sweeney, the San Diego veterinarian who runs the Hyatt Waikoloa swim-with-dolphin programme in Hawaii, to secure the animals.

Sweeney's first attempts to take the dolphins from Charlotte Harbour in south-west Florida in August 1989 were unsuccessful – no dolphins were to be found and the capture boats were continually hounded by a Sea Shepherd team, led by Ben White.

The Sea Shepherd Society has long opposed the capture of wild dolphins, and their relentless pursuit of the captors for the Baltimore Aquarium has raised the intensity of the dolphin debate in Florida, many of whose residents are unhappy about supplying dozens of dolphins from their coastal waters each year, committing them to a premature death in captivity elsewhere. By October 1989, public feeling was running high, and a Florida congressman, Republican Porter Goss, asked the NMFS to suspend the Baltimore Aquarium's permits. Goss said that the NMFS estimate of 250 animals for the Charlotte Harbour dolphin population was outdated, and that more recent government counts indicated that there were only 117 dolphins in the area.

Despite the growing local opposition, the aquarium pressed ahead with its plans, and in late November their team successfully captured two male bottlenose dolphins – not in Charlotte Harbour, but in Tampa Bay, 150 km (95 miles) north. Sweeney's federal permit allowed him to capture up to nine dolphins anywhere along the Gulf Coast, but the state permit needed to move the dolphins specified that they could be moved only from Charlotte Harbour.

Nevertheless, with the approval of the Baltimore Aquarium Director Nicholas Brown, the dolphins were trucked to the Florida Keys, where they were placed in a holding pool at the Hawk's Cay resort in the Florida Keys. State officials were furious, and Governor Bob Martinez called for the pressing of criminal charges against the aquarium. The Governor also offered to provide state transfer permits for any other dolphins caught, if the two captive dolphins were released.

The offer was declined by Brown, who told the local media that the Baltimore Aquarium did not want to rent or buy other dolphins because they could not be bred successfully, and wild captures are less expensive. The two dolphins are still being held in Hawk's Cay, and have become the focus of intense legal and political debate. Their holding pen has been the site of protest activity which has kept the issue in the public eye.

Conservationists are hopeful that whatever is the final outcome for the two captive dolphins, the Baltimore Aquarium's ability to capture dolphins will have been seriously damaged. Says Ben White: "I consider this whole event to have been the watershed event for the issue of capturing dolphins.... it will be difficult for the Baltimore Aquarium or anyone else to capture dolphins. We have shown that dolphins belong in the wild."

# 13: THE MILITARISATION OF FLIPPER

The US Navy first turned its attention to the military potential of dolphins and other marine mammals some 30 years ago. At first the design features of dolphins intrigued the Navy, and studies began in 1960 with the Pacific white-sided dolphin to try to learn hydrodynamic lessons which could then be applied to the development of new torpedoes. As the experiments progressed, the Navy became more interested in dolphins' ability to detect and classify a wide range of targets through the use of their sonar system. The dolphins' large brain, co-operative nature, and complex range of behaviour opened up all sorts of potential for their use in the war industry. According to US Navy budgets, nearly US$30 million was spent on its marine mammal programme between 1985 and 1989, a programme euphemistically called "advanced marine biological systems." About 130 animals are now enrolled with the US military, mostly bottlenose dolphins, but also beluga whales and sea lions.

The dolphins serve as subjects for applied research. Their bodies sometimes provide a perfect model of streamlining for movement in water and their echolocation system displays a sophisticated mechanism for the transmission and reception of sound and vibration over great underwater distances. Cetaceans and other mammals are also trained to carry out specific missions. Project Quick Find, which has been under development since 1975, trained sea lions to retrieve re-usable items of test weaponry from the seabed by homing in on acoustic beacons attached to the weapons. Sea lions can only dive to depths of 160 metres (520 feet) or so, so Project Deep Ops was developed as a complement, using pilot and killer whales to recover lost test torpedoes from as deep as 530 metres (1720 feet). The retrieval capabilities of belugas, which can dive in excess of 700 metres (2275 feet), have also been tested.

Quick Find was not considered by the Navy to be a secret activity. Other projects most certainly are but some information has, nevertheless, managed to find its way into the open. One of the most sensitive projects underway is the training of dolphins to guard US ships – the so-called "swimmer nullification" programme. In 1971, the Navy dispatched a team of dolphins to Vietnam, to guard its fleet based at Cam Ranh Bay from saboteurs. In 1976, a key member of the Navy dolphin project told a Senate Committee that the dolphins were "armed" with large carbon dioxide-filled hypodermic needles strapped to their beaks. They had been previously taught to hunt out any human swimming in the water and to prod them with their beaks. The dolphins would thereby, in all innocence, be giving the "enemy" swimmer or diver a massive and fatal injection of gas into their lungs or stomach.

Dolphins are now being promoted to play a similar kind of guard role for the Navy's nuclear deterrent. A public notice filed in June 1988 by the US Army Corps of Engineers announced plans to construct 16 underwater pens at the Bangor Naval Submarine Base, home of the Trident nuclear missile submarines, in Puget Sound, Washington State. These are intended to house dolphins which will serve as underwater "watchdogs" for the eight huge nuclear submarines.

Objections to the use of dolphins to protect the Navy base are primarily founded on ethical considerations, but another major concern is that dolphins are not always as predictable and reliable as might be expected. US Navy officials acknowledge that dolphins have occasionally gone absent without leave, or have refused to obey orders. But they say that what the animal lacks in discipline, it more than makes up for in sonar and speed.

Mine-detecting is another task allocated to dolphins. Six animals were flown to the Persian Gulf in 1987 to seek out Iranian anti-shipping mines, and to protect the Navy's floating command post from attack by underwater saboteurs.

The US Navy wants to expand its research on dolphins and its use of cetaceans. In March 1988, the Chief of Naval Research told the House of Representatives Appropriations Subcommittee on Defence that military dolphins will be used in "expanding roles", and claimed that the Soviets were attempting to catch up with the US Navy in such research.

While the Naval Ocean Systems Center in San Diego maintains its current policy of not providing briefings and interviews on its research, the full details of the activities for which dolphins are being trained will remain secret.

For some people enough facts have already been revealed for direct action to be taken to oppose the military use of dolphins. In May 1988, someone describing themselves as "Charley Tuna" cut the nets around four of the San Diego dolphin enclosures. In an impressive display of loyalty (or the effects of brainwashing), however, the five released dolphins stayed nearby and swam back into their enclosures the next morning, after trainers came by and repaired their nets.

A subsequent attempt to halt the military use of dolphins, this time through legal action, has had more encouraging results. In 1989, led by the US group the Progressive Animal Welfare Society (PAWS), 15 environmental and animal rights groups brought a lawsuit applying for an injunction against the US Navy's plans to deploy Atlantic bottlenose dolphins at the Trident submarine base at Bangor.

The first main point of contention was the likely effects of bringing dolphins accustomed to the warm waters of Florida or California, where the Navy trains its dolphins, to the chilly waters of Puget Sound. A dolphin had died of a heart attack in 1988, just 11 days after being transported from Hawaii. PAWS contended that moving dolphins to guard the submarine base constitutes a "major federal action" under the National Environmental Policy Act. Such an action requires either an environmental assessment report or a full environmental effect statement, with formal public hearings, before the project can proceed.

The Navy had conducted an environmental assessment of the effects of constructing the 16 holding pens for the dolphins, and their lawyers contended that the law did not require an assessment of the impact of the project on the dolphins themselves. Seattle Federal Judge John Coughenour disagreed with the Navy's submission, and found in favour of the conservationists.

The second main point of contention is an obscure amendment in the Defence Authorisation Act in 1987 that allows the Navy to collect 25 marine mammals each year for "national defence purposes" without the permits required under the MMPA, and outside the guidelines set down in the Act. The conservationists claimed that whether or not the Navy was exempted from the usual application procedures, the capture of dolphins is sufficiently controversial to require public hearings. The judge again found in their favour: "The fundamental problem with the Navy's analysis is that it does not provide for review under the National Environmental Policy Act....yet the controversial decision to take dolphins from the wild for military use is clearly a major federal action with an effect on the environment."

Mitchell Fox of PAWS hailed the decision as a landmark judgement, claiming that conservationists are now close to shutting down the Pentagon's dolphin supply.

**Dolphins that are press-ganged into service with the US Navy are captured in the Gulf of Mexico, and are trained at specialist establishments in the warm waters of Florida, San Diego, or Hawaii. An investigation into the US Navy's training programme by the Marine Mammal Commission uncovered thirteen fatalities from 1986 to 1988. Nearly half the animals were suffering from anorexia or stomach ulcers before their deaths. The Commission urged the Navy to make several changes to its training programme, including less restrictive muzzling of trainee dolphins.**

<blockquote>
**"No sooner does man discover intelligence than he tries to involve it in his own stupidity."**
*Jacques Cousteau*
</blockquote>

The number of dolphins that have died as a consequence of military use is relatively small, yet this exploitative and destructive use of dolphins will increasingly become a target for animal rights activists. One of the main reasons why the US Navy has tried so hard to keep its dolphin work under such heavy wraps is the fear of generating public opposition to its programmes. The idea of using creatures which have become such symbols of peace and harmony to help humans kill each other is a final stroke of black irony.

# PART THREE

**The future for many species of dolphins and small whales looks bleak, but it is not yet too late for positive action to reverse present trends. International and domestic laws can provide for increased protection, and conservation initiatives by both groups and individuals provide inspiration and pressure for change.**

---

# 14: INTERNATIONAL LAW FOR PROTECTING DOLPHINS AND SMALL WHALES

There is no international convention to protect dolphins and other small cetaceans. Small whales and dolphins are massacred in their millions, and for many species the numbers killed have actually been on the increase. In fact the number of small cetaceans now dying at human hands each year is at least five times the number of great whales killed in any year, even when whaling was at its peak.

As a result of conservation efforts dating back over many years, the large whales are now protected under several international laws and by the IWC. But without an international forum or legislation in place to save and protect small whales, dolphins, and porpoises, their wholesale slaughter will continue.

## The International Whaling Commission (IWC)

The IWC was set up in 1946 with a brief to oversee "the orderly development of the whaling industry." Until then, commercial whaling had been killing whales for centuries without any international agreements or controls. When whaling was resumed after a temporary break during the Second World War, the major whaling nations negotiated a formal agreement to manage whale stocks, called the International Convention for the Regulation of Whaling. This led to the establishment of the IWC, and produced two legal texts.

One was the Convention itself, which remains the single most important treaty for the protection of large cetaceans. Thirty-nine countries have at some stage been party to the Convention, although many of them are not currently members. Regulatory measures established by the Convention include the identification of protected and unprotected species and the setting of open and closed seasons and waters. The Convention applies to whales in general, and does not attempt to define what is meant by a whale, a fact that has subsequently created confusion and often given whaling nations a loophole they can use to escape IWC controls. Regulation is generally limited to the twelve species of great whales originally hunted, with the addition in recent years of the much smaller minke whale.

The second legal agreement is the Schedule to the Convention, which sets out the current regulations on the hunting of whales. These are decided by annual meetings of member nations of the IWC. The Convention cannot be changed without renegotiation of the entire agreement, but the Schedule can be changed by a three-quarters majority vote.

"Man has not yet driven any cetacean species to extinction. This may change, however, and soon. For some species, only a few hundred individuals remain. For others, populations of larger or unknown size may be declining rapidly."

*W F Perrin,*
*Cetacean Specialist Group,*
*International Union for the*
*Conservation of Nature*

Although the text of the Convention did not restrict membership of the IWC, and any country could join as long as it paid its annual subscription, all the members of the IWC in the early years were whaling nations. This bias meant that for the first 25 years of its existence the Commission was primarily a "whalers club", and completely failed either to institute proper management procedures or to set sustainable kill quotas. As a result the populations of almost all species of great whales collapsed during the 1950s and 1960s. This collapse was what really forced most of the whaling nations to cease whaling gradually over the last 20 years – commercial whaling became increasingly uneconomic for all but a few nations simply because only a few large whales were left. Indeed, the minke whale, which is the smallest of the baleen whales, was not considered as a commercial quarry until the mid 1970s, by which time the stocks of many of the larger whale species were verging on extinction.

A turning point for the IWC came during the late 1970s and early 1980s, when conservationists successfully encouraged many non-whaling nations to join the Commission. This new lobby was eventually able to give the Commission some effective powers, and in 1982 it voted for a moratorium on commercial whaling. Many people now feel that the IWC should extend its responsibility and begin looking after small cetaceans. The Commission has, after all, had 40 years' experience with cetaceans, is backed up by a strong legal convention, and has a permanent secretariat and administrative structure.

Several moves have, in fact, been made in recent years to try to make the IWC take responsibility for small cetaceans, but member countries have always successfully blocked the proposal. IWC nations like Japan and Denmark are extremely reluctant to have any controls placed on their killing of dolphins and small whales, despite increasing condemnation from the international community. Other countries, such as Mexico, with its huge annual dolphin kill from tuna purse-seining, are concerned that accepting IWC management over small cetaceans would result in loss of control over their 200-mile fishing zones, within which most of the directed hunts for small cetaceans take place, and most of the incidental catches occur.

Countries opposed to bringing small cetaceans under the control of the IWC are using a little-known document produced at the 1946 Conference to back up their efforts to protect their own dolphin-killing interests. The document is known as the "Nomenclature of Whales to the Final Act of the 1946 International Whaling Conference" and was produced by the Secretariat because different delegations were using a variety of names to describe the same species of whales. In an attempt to prevent confusion, the Secretariat produced a list of the twelve species of great whales then commonly hunted, with their local names in each member country.

Now nations like Japan, Mexico, and Denmark are trying to set this up as a definitive list of the whales which come under the regulatory powers of the Commission. Many other IWC members, however, take the view that this "Nomenclature" was intended merely to clarify the confusion over names of whales, and has no legal status. In the debate on this issue at the IWC's Annual Meeting in Sweden in 1985, New Zealand, Australia, the Netherlands, Sweden, the United Kingdom, and Finland all voiced this opinion. They were however, opposed by a greater number of states who did not wish to see the IWC directing the management of dolphins and small whales in their Exclusive Economic Zones.

As a result the IWC is left with ridiculous anomalies in terms of what it can and cannot protect. Minke whales, for instance, are an example of a species which was not included on the original list. In subsequent years they became the mainstay of commercial whaling once the larger species had been overexploited and nearly wiped out.

Several countries have attempted to bring the management of dolphins and small whales under the control of the IWC, but the only significant achievement has been the establishment of the Small Cetacean Subcommittee of the IWC's Scientific Committee. Although this Subcommittee receives and discusses a great deal of important information on the status of numerous populations of small whales and dolphins, it is restricted in its authority, and, unlike most of the other IWC subcommittees, cannot set quotas or recommend management procedures to the Commission.

The Small Cetacean Subcommittee is frustratingly powerless, but it has provided a valuable forum through which the plight of many lesser-known dolphin species has been more widely publicised. The hunting of Commerson's and Chilean black dolphins for crab bait in Argentina and Chile, for example, was first brought to international attention at the 1982 meeting of the IWC Scientific Committee.

Occasionally, small cetacean issues reach the conference floor of the Commission, the Faroe Islands pilot whale hunt being an example. If Faroese pilot whaling was subjected to the same regulations as hunts for the larger whale species, the *grynd* would undoubtedly not be permitted to continue without more humane killing methods and the provision of far more scientific data. But because so many members of the IWC are opposed to the Commission being the agency responsible for the management of small cetaceans, only non-binding recommendations have been made to the Danish Government.

Some conservationists believe that the IWC may not be the best protective agency for small cetaceans. They argue that the IWC has developed to deal with the management of directed hunts for large whales, and the many years of whaling operations have provided a considerable amount of information on both the hunts and the whales involved. The information available on most dolphin populations is so poor by comparison that few scientists are prepared to confidently propose management strategies. And in terms of being able to provide effective protection for endangered species, the IWC still has serious shortcomings. For instance, even when the Commission is able to impose unpalatable measures on some of its members, there is always the notorious "90-day rule", which allows any member to lodge an objection to any vote within 90 days, and not be bound by it.

## The United Nations Conference on Environment and Development (UNCED)

In June 1992, world leaders gathered in Rio de Janeiro for the Earth Summit, to map out the future relationship between humanity and the life support systems of the planet into the next millenium. (The UNCED process had required four Preparatory Conferences during the preceeding two years.) The conservation of dolphins had featured prominently during the lead-up to Rio, with a New Zealand-led initiative seeking to confirm the IWC as the agency responsible for small cetaceans, pending the convening of a proposed international conference on their future management in 1995.

The whaling nations bitterly opposed this proposal and New Zealand found little support even from conservationist members of the IWC. Because the UNCED required consensus decision-making, a lame compromise resolution was finally agreed, which acknowledged the IWC as the sole international management agency for large whales and urged all nations to work together for the conservation of small cetaceans. An opportunity to secure a safer future for the world's dolphins through a comprehensive international agreement was lost, perhaps for the rest of the century.

# International Agreements that Provide Limited Protection for Small Cetaceans

## UNITED NATIONS CONVENTION ON
## THE LAW OF THE SEA 1982 (UNCLOS)

The Law of the Sea Convention deals with a great range of issues relating to the use of the world's oceans for navigation, exploitation of marine living resources and minerals, and the sovereign rights of coastal states. It was through UNCLOS that the 200-mile Exclusive Economic Zones (EEZs) were established around coastal states.

Article 65 of UNCLOS deals with marine mammals and provides for their co-operative management within EEZs as follows: "States shall co-operate with a view to the conservation of marine mammals and in the case of cetaceans shall in particular work through the appropriate international organisations for their conservation, management and study."

The regulatory power of the IWC and other international bodies to control the exploitation of small cetaceans in EEZs may be enhanced by coastal states through the other provisions of Article 65, which state that: "Nothing in this Part restricts the right of the coastal state or the competence of an international organisation, as appropriate, to prohibit, limit or regulate the exploitation of marine mammals more strictly than provided for in this Part."

UNCLOS Article 120 applies the principle of management by "appropriate international organisations" to cetaceans on the high seas (that is outside any EEZs). Most countries consider that the IWC is the appropriate international authority, with regional fisheries agreements having a role in managing cetaceans involved in fisheries interaction problems such as incidental catch in purse-seine or gill-nets.

Most species of small cetaceans therefore "fall through the cracks". They do not come under the authority of the IWC except through the purely advisory powers of the Small Cetacean Subcommittee of the Scientific Committee, and they fail to receive adequate protection through the provisions of UNCLOS, which recognises the IWC as the appropriate management agency.

## THE CONVENTION ON INTERNATIONAL TRADE IN ENDANGERED SPECIES (CITES)

During the 1960s, it became obvious that one of the greatest threats to the survival of many species was the enormous international trade in live animals, skins, trophies, and products such as ivory and horn. Concern to prevent continuing depletions of wild animal populations to satisfy the requirements of commerce led to the negotiation of the Convention on International Trade in Endangered Species.

Concluded in Washington in 1973, CITES protects species threatened by international trade, and contains three appendices in which animals are listed according to the degree of threat which they face. Those on the most endangered list (Appendix I) may not be traded for commercial purposes. Special permits are required from both importing and exporting countries before trade can take place. Another list (Appendix II) refers to less endangered species, threatened only if trade is not regulated (see Chapter 1).

All cetaceans are included on the first and second lists, which should in theory provide considerable protection against the adverse effects of international trade. However, any signatory state can object to the listing of any species under CITES and not be bound by the restrictions imposed by the Convention on that species. Japan, for example, has entered a reservation on all types of whales, so it can still keep killing and trading them as much as ever. Another problem with CITES is that

*Spotted dolphins. Cetaceans "see" with sound. Their sonar emits a series of clicks and pings that travel long distances through water. When sound waves hit an object, echoes are bounced back to the dolphin, enabling it literally to hear distance, shape, density and even texture.* Bob Talbot

**Above**: A dusky dolphin plays and performs for thrilled visitors at Kaikoura, New Zealand. Watching dolphins and whales in the wild is becoming an increasingly popular pastime throughout the world, and provides an opportunity to enjoy dolphins without putting them through the trauma of captivity.  Barbara Todd

**Opposite**: Spotted dolphins ascending at speed before making a spectacular high leap into the air.  Bob Talbot

**Left**: Bottlenose dolphins like these have been trained by the US Navy for more than 30 years to carry out such operations as "swimmer nullification", where dolphins are taught to prod saboteur divers with gas-filled hypodermics strapped to their beaks. James Watt

*Dolphins are graceful and streamlined swimmers, and commonly travel at speeds greater than 45 km an hour (30 mph). They often jump right out of the water while swimming, enabling them to breathe without losing speed.* Bob Talbot

*Above*: Common dolphins travelling at speed can empty and refill their lungs in just one-fifth of a second, barely breaking the surface as they do so. When diving, they can hold their breath for up to five minutes.  Bob Talbot

*Opposite*: Spotted dolphins surfacing for breath. Cetaceans do not breathe automatically like most mammals, but must breathe consciously. It is thought that only half a dolphin's brain sleeps at a time, because if completely asleep, the dolphin would stop breathing and drown.  Bob Talbot

*Right*: Bottlenose dolphins commonly bear many distinctive scars on their skin. While such marks are often the result of everyday wear and tear, in many cases they are also injuries inflicted deliberately or unwittingly by humans.  Ed Robinson

**Above**: *Small cetaceans like this bottlenose dolphin have come to represent harmony and freedom to humans, yet we continue to kill over a million of them each year.* James Watt

**Left**: *"The dolphin is the only creature who loves man for his own sake ... the dolphin alone ... has no need of any man, yet it is a genial friend to all and has helped many." (Plutarch)* Steve Dawson

by July 1993 only 119 of the world's 240 states had ratified the agreement, and trade in endangered species continues unabated between non-signatories. Until all countries that represent potential markets have ratified the Convention, CITES cannot hope to be fully effective.

## THE CONVENTION ON THE CONSERVATION OF WILDLIFE AND NATURAL HABITATS (THE BONN CONVENTION)

The Bonn Convention was formulated in 1972 and aims at the protection and management of all species that "cyclically and predictably" cross state boundaries. Therefore, it is potentially applicable to most species of dolphins and small whales. The states through which the animals migrate (range states) are required to enter into agreements to conserve threatened species throughout their entire range. Species may be listed on two Appendices. Appendix I lists species presently endangered and requiring protection; Appendix II lists those with an "unfavourable conservation status", which would benefit from international regulation.

The Bonn Convention prohibits "any taking that is not permitted for that species under any other multilateral agreement" (for example, the International Convention for the Regulation of Whaling). Laudable though these objectives are, the Bonn Convention has been ratified by only 26 nations and the European Community. The Convention can become effective only when all the range states conclude agreements for the management and conservation of each species. Over half the membership was reported in 1988 as being behind in its payments to support the secretariat, and the specialist group on small cetaceans was unable to meet for three years because of lack of funds.

## THE BERNE CONVENTION ON THE CONSERVATION OF WILDLIFE AND NATURAL HABITATS

The Berne Convention was concluded in 1979, and is the first to tackle the problem of conserving threatened or endangered migratory species and their habitats. The most threatened species are listed in Appendix II, and require the strictest protection. All important breeding and resting sites are to be covered by the Convention, which also prohibits directed catches for Appendix II species.

Several small cetaceans are covered under Appendix II: common dolphin; bottlenose dolphin; harbour porpoise; whitebeak dolphin; white-sided dolphin; Risso's dolphin; roughtooth dolphin; longfin pilot whale; killer whale; false killer whale.

Breeding and resting areas can be identified easily for many bird species, but implementation of similar provisions for small cetaceans requires the coastal seas of many member states to be designated in their entirety as breeding or resting sites. Other threats to dolphins, such as fishery interactions, food depletion, and marine pollution, are entirely omitted or inadequately addressed.

## OTHER INTERNATIONAL TREATIES

Other treaties could, in theory, be used to address the management of small cetaceans. The African Convention on the Conservation of Nature and Natural Resources, the Permanent Commission of the Conference on the Use and Conservation of the Maritime Resources of the South Pacific, and the Convention on Nature Protection and Wildlife Preservation in the Western Hemisphere, all contain provisions which might be used to incorporate such measures.

In practice these lesser-known treaties are unlikely to provide the global management for small cetaceans so urgently needed. They are for the most part only regional agreements, and lack the broad membership required to address a global conservation problem.

## National Laws

The most effective and detailed measures to protect small cetaceans have been taken at the national level. The Marine Mammal Protection Act (MMPA), enacted by the US in 1972, provides a model for several other states.

The hunting of cetaceans is prohibited in many countries, including Australia, Belize, India, the Netherlands, New Zealand, Seychelles, Sweden, and the United Kingdom. Other countries, such as Brazil and Argentina, have established sanctuary areas to protect endangered species of cetaceans.

National legislation does not always guarantee protection. The provisions of the US MMPA still permit the deaths of thousands of dolphins and porpoises each year in fishing nets. Decrees protecting some dolphin and cetacean species in Peru have not provided a hindrance to the development of the world's second largest directed fishery for dolphins and porpoises.

Nevertheless, national legislation is the only hope for the most endangered species of small cetaceans such as the river dolphins and the vaquita. The rarest animals are usually those with the least widespread distribution, with most or all of their habitat under the control of only one country.

# 15: SAVING DOLPHINS – CONSERVATION INITIATIVES

The imprisonment of the Hawaiian environmentalist Dexter Cate incensed conservation groups throughout the world, but his actions inspired them. The 36-year-old marine scientist and former teacher had been so outraged by the massacre of thousands of dolphins at Iki Island, that one dark night he paddled a small inflatable plastic kayak for a mile through high surf to rescue dolphins trapped in a net and waiting to be slaughtered the next day. Cate went into the bitterly cold water to untie and cut some of the ropes of the nets that imprisoned the dolphins, managing to rescue some 250 of them. Hours later the exhausted Cate was forced ashore by high winds and surf, where next morning he was found by the Japanese fishermen who handed him over to the police.

His actions, and the gruesome photos he took that showed the full horror of the Iki dolphin killings to the world, demonstrate the power of just one individual to effect change. Another American, Sam LaBudde, at great personal risk shot and publicised video footage of both the dolphin slaughters in tuna purse-seine nets and the indiscriminate destruction of marine wildlife in the North Pacific drift-nets. He, too, has been inspirational in the way his courageous and dedicated actions have brought these tragedies to world attention and stimulated political leaders and the public to get out and do something.

Many other individuals throughout the world have been working in the public limelight or quietly behind the scenes to protect dolphins. Some may celebrate and demonstrate the consciousness and intelligence of dolphins, and encourage as many people as possible to encounter and appreciate the qualities of these friendly, intelligent creatures. Others may work at a political level, generating publicity about the dolphins' plight, taking on the industries which are responsible for the problems, and lobbying for legislative protection.

The failure to date of any single international body to adequately provide for the protection of small cetaceans has resulted in a number of initiatives being taken by a number of organisations. They range from the United Nations to non-governmental conservation groups.

## INTERNATIONAL EFFORTS

**The United Nations Environment Programme (UNEP)**, in collaboration with the UN's FAO, the International Union for the Conservation of Nature (IUCN) and the IWC has formulated a Global Plan for the conservation of marine mammals. UNEP is one of the numerous programmes established by the UN and funded by subscriptions from the member nations. The Plan, which was released in 1984, is an ambitious attempt to establish a comprehensive management strategy for all marine mammals. Its long-term objective is to: "promote the effective implementation of a policy for marine mammals which is as widely acceptable as possible among the Governments and people of the world."

The Global Plan identified the major conservation issues facing all marine mammals throughout the world, and proposed a budget of US$12 million to fund the investigations required to provide solutions to the most critical problems. Governments, intergovernmental bodies

> "On February 28,1980, I witnessed an atrocity. I watched as thousands of dolphins met a gruesome agonising death. The suffering was unmistakable. On February 29th I released as many as I could from the confining net, to spare them from a similar fate. I now stand trial for interfering with the fishermen's work."
>
> *Dexter Cate, describing the actions which led to his imprisonment in Japan.*

such as the IWC, and non-governmental organisations such as Greenpeace have been consulted, and invited to co-operate in assisting with the Plan. It was originally envisaged that a full-time secretariat, a planning and co-ordinating committee, and a scientific committee would be established. Unfortunately, financial support for the UNEP initiative has been inadequate, and conservation projects continue to be tackled piecemeal. The Global Plan is still no more than a comprehensive wish-list of worthy programmes awaiting the provision of funding. It is, nonetheless, a valuable background to some of the major conservation issues facing dolphins and other marine mammals. Copies of the Plan can be obtained from:

United Nations Environment Programme
PO Box 30552
Nairobi
Kenya

## CONSERVATION INITIATIVES

**The World Conservation Union, (WCU)**, (formerly the International Union for the Conservation of Nature (IUCN), is an international grouping of several hundred governmental and non-governmental organisations. The Cetacean Specialist Group, currently co-chaired by Stephen Leatherwood and Randall Reeves, has prepared an Action Plan for the Conservation of Dolphins, Porpoises, and Whales. At present, the Action Plan lists 60 projects which the members of the CSG recognise as requiring urgent attention, and is an extremely valuable summary of the status of the world's most threatened small cetaceans.

Many of the projects are in developing countries, focussing in particular on the endangered river dolphins. The Action Plan covers the years 1993-1997, and the CSG is actively seeking funding for the administration and execution of the projects. Between 1990 and 1992, over US$500,000 was raised from a wide variety of organisations and individuals around the world and distributed to the scientists and wildlife managers currently implementing the programmes. A great deal, however, remains to be done — a further US$3 million is required to fully fund all the projects approved so far.

Although a few governments have adopted programmes from the Action Plan as national priorities, for many developing countries, conservation of small cetaceans is low on the agenda. The Action Plan probably represents the most carefully thought-out and comprehensive scheme ever drawn up for the protection and preservation of dolphins and porpoises. Copies can be obtained from:

WCU Publications Service
219c Huntingdon Road,
Cambridge CB3 ODL
England

Price: US$17 plus $1.50 postage

## POLITICAL INITIATIVES

Political initiatives play a significant role in advocating for the protection of small cetaceans.

The European Parliament has debated both the Faroe Islands pilot whale hunt (grynd) and the Eastern Tropical Pacific tuna fishery. It effectively closed down the hunt for harp seal pups by banning the importation of baby seal pelts into the European Community, and brought an end to commercial sperm whaling by prohibiting the importation of sperm whale oil.

At the national level, several countries are taking positive steps to promote the conservation and protection of small cetaceans. Brazil, which was still commercially whaling until very recently, established a marine reserve for spinner dolphins in 1988, at Fernando de Noronha National Marine Park. In December 1988, New Zealand declared a marine mammal sanctuary at Banks Peninsula, covering some 1140 square km (500 square miles), to protect the endangered Hector's dolphin.

In the US, Congresswoman Barbara Boxer guided the Dolphin Protection Consumer Act through the House of Representatives. The legislation provides for the compulsory labelling of tuna so that consumers can tell whether it has been caught by encircling dolphins.

Tuna which is not "dolphin safe" will be banned in the US after June 1994. The International Dolphin Conservation Act, approved by the US Congress in October 1992, sets a deadline of 1 March 1994 for the establishment of a global moratorium on harvesting tuna by setting purse seine nets on dolphins. Tuna fishing nations which do not comply will be subject to an embargo of their fish products by the US.

In November 1989, 22 Pacific Island states and territories signed the Convention to Prohibit Drift-net Fishing in the South Pacific, which established a drift-net-free zone of some 20 million square km (8 million square miles).

The Australian State of Victoria in 1988 passed legislation to prohibit the capture of cetaceans for display, and the Federal Government in 1988 led a diplomatic offensive against the mass slaughter of dolphins by the tuna industry.

## ORDINARY PEOPLE SPEAK OUT

Many groups throughout the world are working for dolphin conservation and protection, and their actions and consciousness-raising work help create a wave of public opinion that pushes governments into action, and puts the heat on companies and countries that continue to exploit dolphins and small whales. Action can take many forms – from education and public awareness campaigns, lobbying in high places in government and boardrooms, raising funds and support for specific conservation projects, through to carrying out long-neglected investigative research.

Some groups are well known, such as Greenpeace, now a large international organisation and skilled in the art of publicity campaigns, high-powered lobbying and pressure tactics. Greenpeace, along with other international organisations such as World Wildlife Fund, contributes money and resources to dolphin conservation projects and education programmes in many countries, as well as providing funding for courtroom battles and research in remote parts of the world. Their single greatest weapon is probably international publicity, and through the columns of newspapers and magazines and via satellite and television, they can reach a huge audience. When Greenpeace took its flagship *Rainbow Warrior* into the Tasman Sea in search of drift-netting boats in January 1990, it aimed not only to record and document the catch of the fleet, but also to bring the issue to world attention. Inviting independent journalists, photographers and film crews on the trip ensured worldwide publicity, and during the campaign, co-ordinator Mike Hagler fielded an endless stream of enquiries and interviews from radio stations and press agencies throughout the world. At the height of

All the prime meat from whales killed in Iceland's whale research studies was shipped to Japan, a trade worth about US$50 million in 1987. Fish is Iceland's major foreign exchange earner, accounting for 70 per cent of her exports, including US$200 million annually from the US. A Greenpeace-led US consumer boycott of Icelandic fish was estimated in February 1989 to have cost Iceland more than US$50 million in lost sales, and lost market share in Europe and the US. Several of the largest US fast-food chains reduced or cancelled orders for Icelandic cod and pollock as a result of consumer pressure. The boycott was called off only after Iceland announced an end to its scientific whaling programme in July 1989.

In December 1988, the largest supermarket chain in Austria halted all purchases and sales of yellowfin tuna caught on dolphin. Soon after, the Austrian government banned the import of all such canned yellowfin tuna. Woolworths, a major New Zealand chain store, announced in August 1989 that it would not knowingly stock canned tuna taken in drift-nets, and warned all its major seafood suppliers that future contracts would be promptly cancelled if transgressions of this policy occurred.

*Earthtrust's "Flipper Seal of Approval" on a can of tuna signifies no dolphins have been harmed in the catching of the fish.*

the action, he spent 42 hours constantly handling calls from the media. Drift-net fishing suddenly became a household word, often in countries that had previously been dimly aware of the practice. In West Germany alone, Greenpeace supporters pledged DM7 million to the Greenpeace drift-net campaign during the two weeks of the *Rainbow Warrior's* cruise.

Greenpeace is of course renowned throughout the world for its commitment to non-violent direct action. Other groups and individuals, frustrated by the inertia of political powers, and outraged by the inhumanity of the slaughter or torture of cetaceans, are moved to take more direct action. In 1979, activist members of the group Sea Shepherd rammed the pirate whaling ship *Sierra*, which had been killing hundreds of whales in the North and South Atlantic Oceans for many years. Another Sea Shepherd sabotage action sank two catcher boats of the Icelandic Whaling Fleet while at their moorings, and caused extensive damage to the whale processing factory. These actions took place at the height of the anti-whaling campaign, when feelings were running high. More recently, some environmentalists have turned to "interventionist" tactics to try and save dolphins – Dexter Cate cut nets to free dolphins in Japan, while "Charley Tuna" liberated dolphins from military training enclosures in Hawaii. In these cases, individuals have been prepared to break the law and risk imprisonment for their beliefs.

Well-organised consumer boycotts can also be powerful weapons for change, which conservationists have put to good use. A US Consumer boycott of Icelandic fish , led by Greenpeace, succeeded in stopping Iceland's "scientific whaling" programme. A similar consumer coalition forced the US NMFS to uphold the will of Congress in compelling tuna boats to carry observers, as the result of a successful lawsuit in 1989. Furthermore, the observation and inspection of drift-net vessels operating within US waters has been improved only because of the legal action initiated by environmental groups. The most recent victory has been the consumer boycott of the "tuna caught on dolphin," organised in the USA by a coalition of groups including Greenpeace and the Humane Society, which has persuaded the largest tuna canner in the USA, Starkist, to pledge it will not buy tuna caught in drift-nets or by fishing on dolphins. Earthtrust's "Flipper Seal of Approval," to be used on cans of tuna which have not endangered dolphin in their production, helps consumers exercise their choice for dolphin protection.

Conservation is now becoming an increasingly popular target for corporate sponsorship. The public outcry against drift-nets in New Zealand in 1989, for example, saw one of the country's leading advertising agencies, Colenso, on its own initiative, develop a theme, produce the artwork, and buy the newspaper space for a stunning advertisement opposing drift-netting. Many consumers in the wealthier Western countries are actively seeking to purchase "environmentally-friendly" products. Manufacturers of such products often divert a percentage of sales to supporting projects aimed at protecting the environment or threatened species. Creighton's Naturally, a British-based cosmetics company, which uses all natural products, provided a sophisticated computer package to be used in the Hector's dolphin research programme in New Zealand, where the company was trying to increase its market share. Creighton's has undertaken to set aside a small percentage of the money received from each item it sells, to be put towards conservation projects. Consumers can therefore make an active choice to support conservation initiatives while doing their shopping.

Conservation initiatives aimed at the protection of marine mammals can often be expressed at a very practical level. Project Jonah has for many years led the way in dealing successfully with the many and frequent strandings of whales and dolphins around the New Zealand coastline. Besides fund-raising to supply whale rescue pontoons in areas where strandings are common, Project Jonah volunteers are often called out to assist at strandings in their area. The organisation runs its own training courses in whale rescue techniques, and pioneered the development of the custom-made inflatable pontoons now used throughout New Zealand in the rescues of stranded small whales and dolphins.

Many of the city-dwellers whose funds support the groups working for cetacean conservation have never seen a whale or dolphin in the wild, yet they will gladly dig deep into their pockets to assist in efforts to preserve dwindling populations. The 1980s have seen a remarkable upsurge in the marketing of "wilderness experiences" for urbanites. Whale and dolphin watching has developed rapidly, and the revenues generated by such ventures worldwide now exceed those produced by the whaling industry. Tourists flock to Stellwagen Bank off Boston, and to the island of Maui in the Hawaiian Islands, to see the humpback whales. They come in droves to see gray whales at Scammons' Lagoon, Baja California, Mexico . The remote Valdez Peninsula in Argentina attracts astonishing numbers of nature-lovers to see right whales. Monkey Mia, in remote Western Australia, has become a mecca for dolphin-lovers, and in Kaikoura, on the east coast of New Zealand's South Island, the unique combination of the world's largest toothed whale (the sperm whale) and one of the smallest (Hector's dolphin), within a couple of miles of each other, has provided a huge boost to the local economy. Erich Hoyt has published an excellent handbook, *The Whale Watcher's Guide,* for the globetrotting watcher of cetaceans.

In some places, such as the Australian state of Victoria, the increase in the watching of dolphins and whales has resulted in a change in public attitudes, and the banning of dolphin captures or displays.

As many fisheries have declined, and governments have withdrawn money for cetacean research, scientists are increasingly turning to the larger environmental groups to fund expensive field work. The Greenpeace European campaign vessel *Sirius* carried two scientists from the University of Barcelona throughout 1988/89 whose main job was to record sightings of cetaceans. Greenpeace Italy hosted a seminar in July 1989, attracting that country's most eminent cetologists, to develop a protocol for a census of the Mediterranean cetacean populations. Several smaller organisations specialise in funding investigative research into dolphin conservation concerns. Groups based in the UK include the Environmental Investigation Agency and the Whale and Dolphin Conservation Society; in the US similar groups include the International Wildlife Coalition, Earth Island Institute, Earthtrust and the Humane Society.

Some groups concentrate on co-ordinating the work of numerous non-governmental organisations and groups. For example, the Monitor Consortium, based in Washington DC, sends a regular package of press clippings to subscribers, with the most up-to-date news on a wide range of conservation issues, including marine mammals. Annual subscriptions are about US$250.

As an increasing number of people become aware of the precarious situation for many dolphin species, international public opinion may yet force changes in attitudes in boardrooms and governments. Let us hope that the changes will come soon – for some species time is close to running out.

# 16: WHAT YOU CAN DO TO HELP

> "We must make every attempt to prevent their destruction, and ultimately, establish communication with them. If the term 'humanity' is to have any real meaning, we can do no less."
>
> *Dexter Cate,*
> *Hawaiian environmentalist*

The continuing slaughter of intelligent, peaceful dolphins in their thousands is a senseless and shameful massacre. Concern is growing internationally. Even Dr Fukuzo Nagasaki, Director of the Institute of Cetacean Research, which is currently dedicated to proving that Japan should be allowed to start commercial whaling again, says: "We need to study this now. This is what happened with the whaling industry. The world was too greedy and only began to take notice when it was too late."

Yet little international protection is offered to the great majority of cetacean species. While so much effort has been put into saving the great whales by halting commercial whaling, the deaths of hundreds of thousands of dolphins, porpoises and small whales each year have been continuing unabated, and in many cases have increased significantly in recent years.

It is not too late. But we must raise our voices and act *now*.

The international political community has shown its ability to move swiftly and purposefully (by their standards anyway) to address the destruction of the ozone layer through the negotiation of the Montreal Convention. A similar commitment to purposeful action is now needed to safeguard the world's dolphins and porpoises.

## IMMEDIATE ACTION THAT CAN BE TAKEN TO HELP DOLPHINS

- Most importantly, an international forum must be established where the conservation strategies so urgently needed can be debated and then put into place.

  The battle to save the great whales is still far from finally won, but public opinion can ensure that for those species protected through the IWC, catches will be nil or very low for many years to come.

  Now dolphins and small whales urgently need similar protection in international law.
- Regional fisheries agreements and marine resource conventions should provide effective conservation measures for dolphins and small cetaceans. We must no longer accept the traditional view that marine ecosystems are important only for their stocks of commercially exploited fish and shellfish species. Maintenance of the ecological balance must become the fundamental objective of all fisheries management.
- The giant US tuna canners must be held to their new policy of handling only dolphin-safe tuna. Amendments to the US MMPA to prohibit the practice of encircling dolphins to catch tuna, whether by US or foreign vessels supplying the US market, must be enforced.
- All countries importing tuna must ban the imports of tuna caught on dolphin. Consumers should demand that laws be enacted to carry this out.
- Countries like Peru, which have responded to international pressure and banned the killing of dolphins should be encouraged to ensure compliance with new laws.
- Crab fishing companies in Chile must make a commitment to supplying their vessels with adequate fish bait.
- Nations throughout the world should restrict or ban the use of gill-nets, in coastal seas and on the open ocean. Most gill-netted fish can

be taken by other methods of fishing, which are generally far more selective, and have much less impact on non-target species.
- The UN must ensure compliance with the global ban on drift-netting on the high seas which took effect on 1 January 1993.
- Governments should restrict their nationals from using large-scale drift-nets within their fishing zones, and instruct their canneries to refuse to handle fish caught with drift-nets, as has happened in the South Pacific.
- International agreements such as MARPOL, which governs marine pollution, could be far more effectively enforced. If all the shipping nations faithfully adhered to the spirit and letter of the MARPOL agreement and its five annexes, the world's oceans would undoubtedly provide a much better habitat for all marine wildlife.

## LOBBYING

Individuals can achieve a great deal by lobbying their elected representatives and becoming involved in the campaigns of various environmental groups. Write letters, visit your politicans and people of power and influence in your community, and press for the changes which will help protect dolphins.

Some of the groups who are actively working for the conservation of marine mammals are:

**American Cetacean Society**
PO Box 2639
San Pedro
California CA 90731
USA

**Center for Coastal Studies**
PO Box 826
Provincetown
MA 02657
USA

**Cetacean Society International**
190 Stillwood Drive
Wethersfield
Connecticut  CT 06109
USA

**CODEFF**
(Comite Nacéional Pro
Defensa de la Fauna y Flora)
Casilla 3675
Santiago
Chile

**Defenders of Wildlife**
1244 19th Street NW
Washington  DC 20036
USA

**Dolphin Action and
Protection Group**
PO Box 227
Fish Hoek 7975
South Africa

**Earthtrust**
2500 Pali Highway
Honolulu 96817
Hawaii
USA

**Earth Island Institute**
Suite 28
300 Broadway
San Francisco
California 94133
USA

| | |
|---|---|
| **Environmental Investigation Agency** | 208/209 Upper St<br>London N1-1RL<br>United Kingdom |
| **Humane Society of the United States** | 2100 L Street NW<br>Washington DC 20037<br>USA |
| **International Wildlife Coalition** | PO Box 388<br>N. Falmouth<br>MA 02556<br>USA |
| **The Monitor Consortium** | 1506 19th Street, NW<br>Washington, DC 20036<br>USA |
| **Project Interlock** | Wade and Jan Doak<br>PO Box 20<br>Whangarei<br>New Zealand |
| **Project Jonah** | PO Box 31 357<br>Milford, Auckland,<br>New Zealand |
| **Sea Shepherd Foundation** | Paul Watson<br>Box 68446<br>Vancouver BC V7X 1A2<br>Canada |
| or | PO Box 7000-S<br>Redondo Beach<br>California CA 90227<br>USA |
| **Union de los Amigos de los Animales** | Godofredo Stutzin<br>Casilla 3675<br>Santiago<br>Chile |
| **Whale and Dolphin Conservation Society** | 20 West Lea Road<br>Bath BA1 3RL<br>Avon<br>United Kingdom |
| **Whale Rescue Centre** | Room 16, 37 Swanson Street<br>Melbourne<br>Victoria 3000<br>Australia |

A number of groups have widespread memberships and branches in many countries. You can find out if they are represented in your country by contacting the Head Offices:

| | |
|---|---|
| **Greenpeace International** | Keizersgracht 176<br>1016 DW<br>Amsterdam<br>Netherlands |
| **Worldwide Fund for Nature (WWF) International** | CH 1196<br>Gland<br>Switzerland |

| | |
|---|---|
| **World Society for the Protection of Animals** | 106 Jermyn Street<br>London SW1 6EE<br>United Kingdom |
| **Friends of the Earth** | 26–28 Underwood Street<br>London N1 7JQ<br>United Kingdom |
| **International Fund for Animal Welfare** | 35 Boundary Road<br>St John's Wood<br>London NW8 0JE<br>United Kingdom |
| **Beauty Without Cruelty** | 57 King Henry's Walk<br>London N1 4NH<br>United Kingdom |

If you feel moved to help prevent the continuing decline of the world's dolphins and other small cetaceans, please make the effort to get involved with the groups working on the issue in your area or country. Voluntary organisations rely on donations of money and time by their supporters, and in many instances achieve remarkable results. For many small cetaceans, the situation has never been more desperate, and the need for concerted pressure for a better future has never been greater.

# APPENDIX: SPECIES LIST

## LIST OF SPECIES

Biologists classify animals and plants according to the degree of similarity they bear to each other. Mammals, birds, reptiles, amphibians and fish are grouped together in the phylum Vertebrata. Within the Class Mammalia, dolphins, porpoises and whales belong together in the order Cetacea. The 77 species of Cetacea fall into two main groups – the baleen whales or Mysticetes (11 species) and the toothed whales or Odontocetes (66 species). The Odontocetes comprise one very large whale (the sperm whale) and two closely-related smaller species, 18 species of rare medium-sized whales (the beaked whales), eight species of small whales and 39 species of dolphins and porpoises.

In this book, we have included not only the true dolphins, but also several other species of Odontocetes, which are more commonly referred to as small cetaceans. Pilot whales, narwhal, beluga and orca suffer many of the same indignities at human hands as do the dolphins. They too are harpooned, driven ashore, caught in nets and poisoned by industrial pollution of their waters.

We have not included the great whales, to whom many books have been devoted, nor the beaked whales – a little-known group of Odontocetes.

The following classification of the dolphins and closely-related species of Odontocetes follows that used by the IUCN Cetacean Specialist Group. For a more detailed classification, see Perrin (*IUCN Action Plan for the Conservation of Biological Diversity in Small Cetaceans*).

### SUPERFAMILY PLATANISTOIDEA (RIVER DOLPHINS)

#### Family Platanistidae:

| | |
|---|---|
| *Platanista gangetica* | Ganges susu |
| *Platanista minor* | Indus River dolphin |

#### Family Pontoporiidae:

| | |
|---|---|
| *Lipotes vexillifer* | baiji, Yangtze River dolphin |
| *Pontoporia blainvillei* | franciscana, La Plata dolphin |

#### Family Iniidae:

| | |
|---|---|
| *Inia geoffrensis* | boto, Amazon River dolphin |

### SUPERFAMILY DELPHINOIDEA

#### Family Monodontidae

| | |
|---|---|
| *Monodon monoceros* | narwhal |
| *Delphinapterus leucas* | beluga |

## Family Phocoenidae (Porpoises)

| | |
|---|---|
| *Phocoena phocoena* | harbour porpoise |
| *Phocoena spinnipinnis* | Burmeister's porpoise |
| *Phocoena sinus* | vaquita |
| *Neophocoena phocaenoides* | finless porpoise |
| *Australophocoena dioptrica* | spectacled porpoise |
| *Phocoenoides dalli* | Dall's porpoise |

## Family Delphinidae (Dolphins and Small Whales)

### Subfamily Orcaellinae:

| | |
|---|---|
| *Orcaella brevirostris* | Irawaddy dolphin |

### Subfamily Steninae – Hump-backed dolphins:

| | |
|---|---|
| *Steno bredanensis* | rough-toothed dolphin |
| *Sousa chinensis* | Indopacific hump-backed dolphin |
| *Sousa teuszii* | Atlantic hump-backed dolphin |
| *Sousa fluviatilis* | tucuxi |

### Subfamily Delphininae – Dolphins:

| | |
|---|---|
| *Lagenorhynchus albirostris* | white-beaked dolphin |
| *Lagenorhynchus acutus* | Atlantic white-sided dolphin |
| *Lagenorhynchus obscurus* | dusky dolphin |
| *Lagenorhynchus obliquidens* | Pacific white-sided dolphin |
| *Lagenorhynchus cruciger* | hourglass dolphin |
| *Lagenorhynchus australis* | Peale's dolphin |
| *Grampus griseus* | Risso's dolphin |
| *Tursiops truncatus* | bottlenose dolphin |
| *Stenella frontalis* | Atlantic spotted dolphin |
| *Stenella attenuata* | pantropical spotted dolphin |
| *Stenella longirostris* | spinner dolphin |
| *Stenella clymene* | clymene dolphin |
| *Stenella coeruleoalba* | striped dolphin |
| *Delphinus delphis* | common dolphin |
| *Lagenodelphis hosei* | Fraser's dolphin |

### Subfamily Lissodelphinae – right whale dolphins:

| | |
|---|---|
| *Lissodelphis borealis* | northern right whale dolphin |
| *Lissodelphis peronii* | southern right whale dolphin |

### Subfamily Cephalorhynchinae:

| | |
|---|---|
| *Cephalorhynchus commersonii* | Commerson's dolphin |
| *Cephalorhynchus eutropia* | Chilean black dolphin |
| *Cephalorhynchus heavisidii* | Heaviside's dolphin |
| *Cephalorhynchus hectori* | Hector's dolphin |

### Subfamily Globicephalinae – small whales:

| | |
|---|---|
| *Peponocephala electra* | melon-headed whale |
| *Ferusa attenuata* | pygmy killer whale |
| *Pseudorca crassidens* | false killer whale |
| *Orcinus orca* | killer whale |
| *Globicephala melas* | long-finned pilot whale |
| *Globicephala macrorhynchus* | short-finned pilot whale |

# GLOSSARY

**ATA – American Tunaboat Association**. A powerful lobby group representing US tuna interests. The US demand for tuna is 45 per cent of the total global consumption, but only 1 per cent of the world catch is taken within US waters. American tunaboats, and their processing companies and canneries, range throughout the South Pacific.

**CITES – Convention for International Trade in Endangered Species**. International agreement governing the trading of endangered species for profit (see Chapter 14).

**Drift-net**. A gill-net which may be up to 60 km (38 miles) in length and 15 metres (50 feet) deep, set to drift through the upper layers of the open ocean to entrap fish, especially tuna and salmon, or squid. Marine mammals and sea birds are regular casualties of drift-nets.

**Drive fishery**. A method of catching dolphins and small whales, in which a number of boats gather together to drive the animals towards shore by generating underwater noise – often a long metal pole struck by a hammer or rock. The dolphins swim away from the noise; even when close to the beach, very few will try to break through the noise barrier. The animals are generally killed with knives or lances in shallow water or on shore.

**EEZ – Exclusive Economic Zone**. One of the most important consequences of the UNCLOS agreement was the establishment of 200-nautical mile (370-km) zones, within which the coastal state has sovereignty over fisheries resources.

**ETP – Eastern Tropical Pacific**. Some 11 million square km (6 million square miles) of Eastern Pacific Ocean, mainly off the west coasts of Central and northern South America, in which yellowfin tuna frequently associate with dolphins. The major commercial purse-seine fishery in the ETP has killed many millions of dolphins in recent years.

**FAO – Food and Agriculture Organisation of the United Nations**. The UN agency responsible for compiling international fisheries data and providing advice to national agencies; particularly concerned with fisheries in developing countries.

**FFA – Forum Fisheries Agency**. The South Pacific nations' fisheries agency, with headquarters in Honiara, Solomon Islands, which negotiates with distant-water fishing nations wishing to fish in the South Pacific.

**Gill-net**. A net usually made of nylon mesh, which traps fish by entangling them through the bony plate surrounding the gills. Gill-nets may be anchored (set-nets) or allowed to drift through the upper layers of the deep open ocean (drift-nets).

**IATTC – Inter-American Tropical Tuna Commission**. The international body responsible for management of tuna stocks in the ETP. The Commission has only limited powers, and as a consequence, not only have dolphins died in their millions in the yellowfin tuna fishery, but tuna stocks have also declined below sustainable levels.

**ICCAT – International Council for the Conservation of Atlantic Tunas**. A grouping of Atlantic nations and distant-water fishing nations which is the management agency for all species of tuna in the North and South Atlantic Ocean.

**IUCN – International Union for the Conservation of Nature**. A global coalition of non-governmental and inter-governmental conservation organisations, with headquarters in Gland, Switzerland. Much of the funding for IUCN has been provided by the WWF, and it acts as a valuable focus for international conservation initiatives.

**IWC – International Whaling Commission**. An international organisation responsible for the management of the world's whales. Originally formed as a whalers' club to divide up kill quotas, the IWC became increasingly dominated by conservationist nations during the 1970s and early 1980s. Many members refuse to recognise the IWC's competence to manage small cetaceans, although the Small Cetacean Subcommittee of the IWC Scientific Committee is at present the major international forum to discuss conservation problems for dolphins, porpoises, and small whales.

**Longlining**. A method of fishing in which a number of baited hooks are set to catch fish. Demersal longlines are set on the seabed to catch bottom-living species; pelagic longlines are set in the open ocean, to catch surface-swimming species such as tuna.

**MMPA – Marine Mammals Protection Act**. The first MMPA, and the one on which many others were modelled, was passed in the US in 1972. The US Act still permits the "accidental" capture of marine mammals in fishing operations, but only if the Secretary of Commerce determines that a marine mammal species is not endangered by the incidental kill. Nevertheless, more than 800,000 dolphins have died in US purse-seine fishing since the MMPA came into force.

**NMFS – National Marine Fisheries Service**. The US Government Agency responsible for the administration of the MMPA, as well as the management of fish resources.

**PCBs – Polychlorinated biphenyls**. A group of closely related chemicals which were produced in considerable quantities in the 1950s and 1960s. Only recently has it been discovered that PCBs are extremely toxic to many birds and mammals, especially marine mammals. Because they are chemically very stable, PCBs will continue to pose a threat to marine mammals for many decades to come.

**Purse-seine**. A method of fishing in which a net, up to 2 km (1.25 miles) long and 100 metres (325 feet) deep, is set from a large fishing vessel, with the intention of trapping schools of tuna by sealing (or "pursing") the bottom of the net, preventing the tuna from escaping. The introduction of purse-seiners into the ETP killed millions of dolphins, unwitting casualties of the nets.

**Rolling hook fishery**. Popular fishing method used in the Yangtze River, in which groups of large unbaited hooks are placed on the river bed, with the intention of impaling catfish. The major source of incidental mortality of the world's rarest dolphin, the Baiji, whose total population is estimated at only 200–300. Half of the 100 or so dolphins found dead between 1950 and 1980 had died from swallowing or being impaled upon rolling hooks.

**Trawling**. A method of fishing in which a net is towed behind the vessel, either along the bottom (bottom trawling), or at some depth above the bottom (midwater trawling).

**Trolling**. A fishing method in which a number of lures are trailed behind the vessel, usually to catch species of tuna.

**UNCLOS – United Nations Convention on the Law of the Sea**. The Law of the Sea took many years to negotiate, and is yet to be fully ratified by all the UN nations. Nevertheless, many of the key provisions of UNCLOS, such as the establishment of EEZs, rights of innocent passage, and the conservation and management of migratory species, have become customary international law.

**WWF – Worldwide Fund for Nature**. Formerly known as the World Wildlife Fund, WWF is one of the world's most effective conservation organisations. WWF probably raises more money for conservation projects each year than any other group. A considerable proportion of its funds in the past have gone to support IUCN, and the Fund has assisted in a great many dolphin conservation programmes all over the world.

# REFERENCES

This is by no means an extensive list of references, but rather a selection of the most valuable or accessible documents, articles, and papers. The regular newsletters of Greenpeace, Earthtrust, and Earth Island Institute have also been of great value in compiling this book, as have numerous reporters all over the world whose work has been distributed through the Monitor Consortium network.

**CHAPTER 1**
(These references are also extensively used throughout the text)
The Global Plan for the Conservation and Management of Marine Mammals: United Nations Environment Programme.
Dolphins, Porpoises and Whales. An Action Plan for the Maintenance of Biological Diversity, 1988–1992: Cetacean Specialist Group, IUCN H.W. Perrin (ed.).
Newsletters of the Cetacean Specialist Group of IUCN. H.W. Perrin, (ed.).
*Whales of the World*. Lyall Watson, Hutchinson, 1981.

**CHAPTER 2**
*Mind in the Waters*. Joan McIntyre, (ed.), Sierra Club Books, 1974.
*Encounters with Whales and Dolphins*. Wade Doak, Hodder and Stoughton, 1988.
*Save the Dolphins*. Horace Dobbs, Souvenir Press, 1981.

**CHAPTERS 3 and 4**
*The Mind of the Dolphin*. John Lilly, Avon Books, 1969.
*The Natural History of Whales and Dolphins*. Peter G.H.Evans, Christopher Helm, 1987.
*Research on Dolphins*. Harrison and Bryden, Oxford University Press, 1986.
*Dolphin, Dolphin*. Wade Doak, Hodder and Stoughton, 1981. (Published in the USA by Sheridan House.)

**CHAPTER 5**
Biology and Conservation of the River Dolphins. *IUCN Species Survival Commission Occasional Paper no.3*, 1989; Perrin & Brownell (eds).
Slow Boat to Oblivion. Sam LaBudde, *Earth Island Institute Journal*, September 1989.

**CHAPTER 6**
Paper to IWC Scientific Committee, T. Kasuya, 1989.
Exploitation of small cetaceans in coastal Peru. Read, Reyes, van Waerebeek, McKinnon and Lehman, *Biological Conservation 46*, 517–523.
Whale and Dolphin Conservation Society Newsletters. Kieran Mulvaney.
Environmental Investigation Agency Reports. Allan Thornton.

**CHAPTER 7**
*The Tragedy Continues*. Earth Island Institute, San Francisco, 1988.

**CHAPTER 8**
Stripmining the Oceans. Sam LaBudde, Earthtrust, 1989.
Report of observer on board *Monju Maru*, February 1989; R. Goldblatt, Marine Resources Management Division, Colonia, Yap, Federated States of Micronesia, 1989.

## CHAPTER 9

World review of interactions between marine mammals and fisheries. S. Northridge, FAO Fisheries Technical Paper no.251, 1984.
Factors affecting the recovery of the vaquita; J. Barlow, Southwest Fisheries Center Administrative Report LJ 86-37, 1986.
Incidental catch of harbor porpoises by gill nets. Read and Gaskin, *Journal of Wildlife Management 52*: 517-523, 1988.
Can the vaquita be saved?, G.K. Silber, *Defenders*, May/June 1987.
Harbor porpoises and the gill-net fishery, T. Polacheck, *Oceanus*, 32T. 1989.

## CHAPTER 10

Dawson, S. and Slooten, E.: International Whaling Commission, Special Volume on *Cephalorhynchus*, Donovan (ed.)
Public Discussion Document on Conservation of Hector's Dolphin, October 1988, New Zealand Department of Conservation (PO Box 10420, Wellington).
Incidental catch of Hector's dolphins in inshore gill nets. S. Dawson, in press.

## CHAPTER 11

Cummins, J. *The Ecologist, 18*, 1988.
Pierre Beland. *Nature Canada*, Fall 1988.
Marine debris in NZ waters. Department of Conservation, New Zealand, November 1989.

## CHAPTERS 12 and 13 were sourced mainly from newspaper reports.

## CHAPTER 14

The role of law in protecting marine mammals. P. Byrnie, *Ambio*, 1986.
Saving the small cetaceans. N. Meith, *Ambio*, *XIII* (1) 1984.

# INDEX

Killer whale – see orca
Korea 65, 71

**L**

LaBudde, Sam 47, 59, 67, 103
Lifespan 38

**M**

Marine Mammals Protection Act (MMPA) 61, 68, 70, 102
MARPOL 109
Medina panel 60
Melon 30, 54
Mercury 53, 84
Mexico 76
Mirex 82
Monitor Consortium107, 110
Monkey Mia 24–5
Monodontidae 27
Monofilament 44, 65, 74, 78
Myoglobin 34
Mysticetes 27
Mythology 21–2

**N**

Narwhal 13, 35, 53
Nina 24
Noise 85

**O**

Oceanic Research and Communication Alliance 91
Odontocetes 111
Oil 85
Opo 23
Orca 18, 39, 89
Organochlorines 82
Ozone 86, 108

**P**

Pacific white-sided dolphin 66
Peale's dolphin 11, 57
Pelorus Jack 23
Peru 51
Phocoenidae 27
Pilot whale 52
Pippard, Leone 82
Plastic debris 84–5
Polychlorinated biphenyls (PCBs) 53, 81–4
Progressive Animal Welfare Society 95
Project Deep Ops 94
Project Interlock 25–6, 110
Project Jonah 106–8, 110
Project Quick Find 94
Purse-seine 59

**R**

Rescue 25
Right whale dolphin 66
Risso's dolphin 16, 77
River dolphins 35, 41–7

**S**

Sea Shepherd 93, 106, 112
Set-nets – see gill-nets
Sexual behaviour 37
Sexual maturity 37
Skin 33

Skipjack tuna 63
Social structure 37
Sonar – see echolocation
Spinner dolphin 15, 60, 77
Spotted dolphin 15, 60
Squalodontids 27
St Lawrence River 13, 81
Streamlining 33
Striped dolphin 14, 84

**T**

Taiwan 57, 65, 71
Tarawa Declaration 69
Trawling 71
Trolling 73
Tuna bombs 59
Turkey 48, 54–5
Tucuxi 45, 76

**U**

Ultra-violet radiation 86
Union de los Amigos de los Animales 110
United Nations Environment Programme (UNEP) 74, 103–5
United Nations Law of the Sea Convention (UNCLOS) 100
US Navy 94

**V**

Vaquita 10, 76

**W**

Whale and Dolphin Conservation Society 107, 110
Whale and dolphin-watching 107
White-beaked dolphin 36
White whale – see beluga
World Society for the Protection of Animals 111
Worldwide Fund for Nature (WWF) International 110

**Y**

Yangtze River dolphin – see baiji
Yellowfin tuna 59, 63